Strategic Public Private Partnerships

Strategic Public Private Partnerships

Innovation and Development

David J. Maurrasse

Founder and President, Marga Incorporated; Adjunct Research Scholar and Associate Professor, Columbia University, USA

Edward Elgar

Cheltenham, UK • Northampton, MA, USA

Published by
Edward Elgar Publishing Limited
The Lypiatts
15 Lansdown Road
Cheltenham
Glos GL50 2JA
UK

Edward Elgar Publishing, Inc.
William Pratt House
9 Dewey Court
Northampton
Massachusetts 01060
USA

A catalogue record for this book
is available from the British Library

Library of Congress Control Number: 2012949447

This book is available electronically in the ElgarOnline.com Social and Political Science Subject Collection, E-ISBN 978 0 85793 198 6

MIX
Paper from
responsible sources
FSC
www.fsc.org   FSC® C018575

ISBN 978 0 85793 197 9 (cased)

Typeset by Columns Design XML Ltd, Reading
Printed and bound by MPG Books Group, UK

Contents

Acknowledgements

This book is the outgrowth of research at the Program on Strategic Partnerships and Innovation at the Earth Institute at Columbia University. Dr. Steve Cohen, the Earth Institute's Executive Director, approved the creation of the Program in 2010. This book simply would not be possible without Steve Cohen. He has been a tremendous advisor and supporter since I arrived at Columbia in 2000. My role at the University has taken several paths, and Steve has been helpful at every turn. Words cannot adequately express my gratitude to Steve.

The Earth Institute provides valuable financial support that enables the Program on Strategic Partnerships and Innovation's continuous research. The Program was fortunate to have received financial support from other sources, such as Holly Delany Cole and the New World Foundation. This support has been critical.

The research assistants and interns who have worked on various aspects of this book deserve special thanks: Ayelet Haran, Adiel Gavish, Michael Beirnard, and Tomoko Iimura all made major contributions to this book. Their research surfaced the many case examples found in these pages, and informed the entire framing of each chapter. The administrative staff of the Earth Institute should also be acknowledged, as they have helped me navigate facilities, travel, finances, human resources, and more.

The research that led to this book is the culmination of years of evolving theory and practice. The work of my company, Marga Incorporated, has shaped a fair amount of the analysis throughout the book. As the company's work has placed me in an advisory role to actual partnerships around the world, I have taken away a great deal. Marga's many clients throughout the years have certainly informed the thinking in this book on many levels. Of course, Marga's many staff members over the years have been very helpful in numerous ways, particularly in helping me create a space that truly transcends theory and practice. Because I must research and write, I cannot always be in the company. Dr. Cynthia Jones, Marga's CEO and great pillar of consistency, has been tolerant and supportive, and the steady hand that keeps the company moving. I am professionally and personally grateful to Cynthia.

One of Marga's substantial ongoing initiatives, the Anchor Institutions Task Force, with its almost 200 members, has been critical to shaping how partnerships in localities form and evolve. I am grateful on many levels to Dr. Ira Harkavy of the University of Pennsylvania, the Task Force's Chair. Our ongoing communication about the Task Force and the wider conceptual considerations of partnerships has significantly influenced some of the thinking in this book. Ira also served as a focus group participant for this research. All of the focus group participants have made a collective contribution to this project. As representatives of different sectors who have participated in cross sector partnerships, they bring unique insights into the promise and pitfalls of these efforts.

Dr. Peter Kresl of Bucknell University has provided a highly useful forum in the Global Urban Competitiveness Project. Thanks to Peter, I have been participating in these meetings in various parts of the world, presenting on some of the concepts contained in this book. The scholars in these meetings have provided valuable guidance and feedback that have pushed my thinking on the global relevance of this topic and the notion of partnerships. Through this group, I met Edward Elgar, who has created this exciting opportunity to publish on a topic that I have pondered for many years, and provide a truly global readership. I am eternally grateful to Edward individually and to the entire press.

I must always acknowledge my mother – the most consistent supporter of all.

Introduction

Today's world confronts devastating natural disasters, widespread health concerns, pressing environmental emergencies, unstable economies, substantial unemployment, and the overall requirement to meet the needs of a substantial and growing population in a much more urbanized and developed globe. As an increased standard of living for larger segments has been an important developmental goal over recent decades, what happens when a larger cross section of the world's population lives in cities and acquires new tastes and demands? What are appropriate solutions when environmental challenges present sweeping and overarching threats?

These complicated times present two critical inextricably linked pathways. One is stimulated by the need to ensure as much equity, sustainability, and safety as possible across an ever interconnected and increasingly developed world. Concurrently, our times represent a pivotal moment calling for innovation of all types and the development of industries that can produce economic opportunity.

This pivotal moment in world history arrives on the heels of tremendous technological innovation. These advances changed the face of the world, having altered the nature of work and the pace of communication and social change. A shift ensued. Employment opportunities for those with limited formal education and skills gradually diminished. An economic downturn shed light on this new picture. Unemployment skyrocketed and gaps in wealth continued to increase. What will be the source of tomorrow's jobs? What kinds of innovations and industries can stimulate and maintain far-reaching economic opportunity?

Both of these pathways – the continued quest for greater equity and development, and the need for innovation and industry to maintain high standards of living – set the stage for creative thinking and active approaches to harnessing myriad segmented resources for new solutions. Multidimensional and complex challenges call for sophisticated solutions. Existing models of governance are probably not sufficient in surmounting the nature and scope of the obstacles of our future.

Consequently, new strategies for the future are required to respond effectively to social, economic, political, and natural challenges. Additionally, contemporary and future considerations require strategies to innovate proactively. Bluntly, the wellbeing of our global society is dependent on new offensive and defensive strategies. Therefore, society can benefit from altered ways of doing business. These new strategies must transcend established boundaries, and catalyze new forms of cooperation.

All institutions and industries in the public, private, and nongovernmental sectors coexist in an ecosystem. As centuries of development and technological advancement have constructed political, economic, and social structures beyond nature, new forms of interaction evolved. Humanity and the natural world have always been an ecosystem. However, the course of development over the centuries spawned sectors of governance, commerce, and even incorporated systems for civil society.

Institutions are composed of and constructed by people. Therefore, partnerships can only succeed with mutual respect and cooperation between individuals. Institutions define only one aspect of differences between people. The reality of an integrated globe is that people across demographic groups and nations interact more than ever. This level of connection is a tremendous opportunity, and could enhance peace and reconciliation. However, deep-seated sentiments and historical inequalities challenge any pursuit of unity. This is a universal consideration in any form of collaboration.

Different cultural groups have always coexisted in segments, but they were not always seamlessly linked. Nationalism forged new links and political forms, placing disparate groups under singular forms of governance promoting unity around particular behaviors and languages. An industrial revolution designed entirely new forms of segmentation. The technological revolution withered boundaries across segments national, industrial, and otherwise.

Regardless of political and industrial segments, interdependence has remained constant. A corporation's success depends on a market that likely includes a broad cross section of the general public. An independent nation's advancement depends not only on its relationship to its own subjects, but also on a global political sphere and degrees of private sector trade. National and local policies, along with the practices of large corporations, shape day-to-day livelihoods in civil society.

Technology raised the stakes of interdependence. It linked people, increasing the ability to interact across boundaries. The Internet in particular birthed social networks that enable high levels of collaboration regardless of established boundaries.

This landscape, characterized by institutional and political boundaries yet potentially interactive through the ease of crossing boundaries technologically, brings a compelling blend of challenges and opportunities. If connectivity has increased, ostensibly, we can more readily harness resources to respond to disasters and cure diseases. When we can connect across sectors and boundaries, we can benefit from shared thinking that leads to innovation of all forms. This is fertile ground for partnerships.

Cross sector collaboration has proliferated recently. These partnerships are forming and evolving in local contexts and across national lines. They are altering approaches to development and spawning innovation. They represent new ways of doing business, but only in their infancy. These partnerships are emblematic of a shifting global landscape, but they are in fact the seeds of strategies for the future.

Our times require innovative thinking and practice in order to make critical decisions and solve problems. Strategic partnerships that cross the public, private, and nongovernmental sectors are increasingly surfacing as new forms of governance and information exchange. The notion of public private partnerships has developed over recent years. However, the incorporation of organizations representing the voice of civil society is also integral to cross sector partnerships. From nongovernmental organizations (NGOs) at the community level to large established anchor institutions like universities, the engagement of the nongovernmental sector is critical to the effectiveness of cross sector partnerships. Overall, public/private/nongovernmental partnerships can be important vehicles in stimulating innovation as well as addressing the important social concerns of our times. These strategic cross sector partnerships can be both proactive and reactive and can take root in specific places and across boundaries.

In particular places and with respect to specific social concerns, it is important to harness resources that may reside in various disparate sectors and industries. Strategic partnerships have become the vehicles through which various participants combine resources and expertise to solve problems jointly or produce innovations. The idea for this book simultaneously emerged with the concept of the Program on Strategic Partnerships and Innovation at Columbia University's Earth Institute.

The Program was created to conduct focus groups with representatives of different sectors who have been involved in partnerships, and continually investigate manifestations of global strategic partnerships. This book emerges from this research in order to further define the nature, scope, effectiveness, and potential of strategic partnerships. If strategic cross sector partnerships can potentially solve pressing global concerns, then what specifically must we understand about these collaborative pursuits that can increase their effectiveness? What variables shape partnerships' relative ability to operate effectively and achieve their intended results?

PART I

The concept of strategic cross sector
partnerships

1. The emergence of strategic partnerships

The Millennium Development Goals (MDGs) provide an important context, crystallizing the numerous persistent challenges throughout the world, and the magnitude of work to be done. The eight challenges outlined in the MDGs capture pressing circumstances that require extensive cooperation and coordination of resources wherever they are situated. The MDGs were born out of the UN Millennium Declaration, adopted by the leaders of 189 nations in September 2000 at the Millennium Summit held at the UN Headquarters in New York. Presented as a blueprint for development in the twenty-first century, the MDGs commit the international community to a set of eight goals to be achieved by the year 2015. Together, the MDGs form a coherent framework for the entire UN system to collaborate toward shared, common goals. These eight goals are:

1. **Eradicate extreme poverty and hunger**: Between 1990 and 2015, reduce by half the proportion of people living on or below the international poverty line (adjusted to $1.25 in 2008 by the World Bank); achieve full and productive employment and decent work for all, including women and young people; and halve the proportion of people suffering from hunger.
   Progress: Between 1990 and 2005, overall poverty rates in developing regions fell from 46 percent to 27 percent, with progress being sustained in many developing countries. However, an estimated 64 million people have been pushed into extreme poverty as a result of the 2008 economic crisis. Moreover, rapid growth in East Asia, especially China, figures greatly in the reduction of global poverty. Strategies that have been effective at poverty reduction include:
   - Subsidy programs in Malawi and Ghana
   - Investing in agriculture research in Vietnam
   - Innovative finance schemes in Nigeria and Bangladesh
   - Employment programs in Argentina.[1]

2.   **Universal education**: Ensure that children everywhere, boys and girls alike, will be able to complete a full course of primary education.

     Progress: Some of the poorest countries, such as Burundi, Madagascar, Rwanda, Samoa, Sao Tome and Principe, Togo, and the United Republic of Tanzania have achieved or are close to achieving the goal of universal primary education. In Benin, Bhutan, Burkina Faso, Ethiopia, Guinea, Mali, Mozambique, and Niger, considerable progress has been made: between 1999 and 2009, net enrolment ratios in primary school increased by more than 25 percentage points.[2] Educational strategies that have worked well include:

     - Abolishing school fees in Burundi, Ethiopia, Ghana, Kenya, Mozambique, Malawi, Nepal, and Tanzania
     - Investing in teaching infrastructures and resources in Ghana, Nepal, and Tanzania
     - Promoting education for girls in Botswana, Egypt, and Malawi
     - Expanding access to remote and rural areas in Bolivia and Mongolia.[3]

3.   **Gender equality**: Eliminate gender disparity in primary and secondary education preferably by 2005, and in all levels of education by no later than 2015.

     Progress: The ratios of enrolment of girls to boys in primary and secondary schools have improved in developing regions, from 91 girls to every 88 boys in 1999 to 96 girls for every 100 boys. However, despite progress, unequal access persists in many parts of the developing world.[4] Progress toward gender equity has been aided by:

     - Providing secondary school stipends for girls in Bangladesh
     - Furthering women's empowerment in Mexico
     - Setting a gender quota for Parliament in Kyrgyzstan.[5]

4.   **Child health**: Reduce by two-thirds the under-five child mortality rate between 1990 and 2015.

     Progress: Between 1990 and 2009, deaths of children under the age of five declined from 12.4 million to 8.1 million.[6] Improved immunization coverage and provision of second-dose immunizations are to thank for the 78 percent drop in death by measles worldwide from 2000 to 2008, accounting for 25 percent of the decline in child mortality on the whole.[7] Child health strategies that have been successful include:

     - Expanding immunization programs in Egypt, Vietnam, and Bangladesh

- Promoting breastfeeding in Cambodia
- Providing mosquito nets in the Republic of Congo, Democratic Republic of Congo, Gabon, Mali, Nigeria, and Zimbabwe.[8]

5. **Maternal health**: Reduce maternal mortality ratio by three-quarters between 1990 and 2015; achieve universal access to reproductive health by 2015.

    Progress: Maternal mortality ratio in the developing world declined from 440 deaths per 100,000 live births in 1990 to 290 maternal deaths in 2008, representing a 34 percent drop. The greatest strides were made in Eastern Asia, Northern Africa, South-Eastern Asia, and Southern Asia. Yet, there is still a long way to go before the MDG target is achieved, and pregnancy continues to be a major health risk for women in several regions.[9] Reduction in maternal mortality is partly due to:

    - Widening access to maternal health services in Egypt
    - Fighting fistula in sub-Saharan Africa, South Asia, and the Arab states
    - Investing in mobile maternal health units in Pakistan.[10]

6. **Combat HIV/AIDS**: Halt and begin to reverse the spread of HIV/AIDS by 2015; achieve universal access to treatment for HIV/AIDS for all those who need it by 2010; and halt and begin to reverse the incidence of malaria and other major diseases by 2015.

    Progress: Since the peak of HIV infections in 1997, the figure declined 21 percent by 2009, with an estimated 2.6 million newly infected people.[11] By the end of 2009, antiretroviral therapy for HIV or AIDS was provided to 5.25 million people in low- and middle-income countries (1.2 million more people since 2008). The number of AIDS-related deaths has declined by 19 percent during this period. However, the improvements have been largely in sub-Saharan Africa and other regions are lagging behind. Various strategies that have worked to reduce the spread of infectious diseases include:

    - Providing free access to antiretroviral treatment in Botswana
    - Slowing new HIV infections among young people
    - Distributing insecticide-treated bed nets against malaria
    - Controlling the incidence of tuberculosis in India
    - Protecting families from malaria, measles, and polio in Togo.[12]

7. **Environmental sustainability**: Integrate the principles of sustainable development into country policies and reverse the loss of environmental losses; reduce biodiversity loss and achieve a significant loss reduction by 2010; halve the proportion of the population

without sustainable access to safe drinking water and basic sanitation by 2015; and achieve a significant improvement in the lives of at least 100 million slum dwellers by 2020.

Progress: The rate of deforestation and loss of forest from natural causes is slowing down, albeit still alarmingly high. Globally, the rate has declined from an estimated 16 million hectares per year in the 1990s to approximately 13 million hectares per year in the 2000s. Progress has been made mainly in Asia (led by China), while South America and Africa continue to lose forests.[13] Although access to improved water, sanitation, or better housing has been made possible for more than 200 million slum dwellers in the past ten years, these slum improvements are not able to keep up with the rapidly growing population of the urban poor. Successful efforts toward environmental progress include:

- Reducing ozone-depleting substances
- Installing water systems in Brazil, Burkina Faso, and Sri Lanka
- Expanding good sanitation practices in Kyrgyzstan.[14]

8. **Global partnership for development**: Develop further an open, rule-based, predictable, nondiscriminatory trading and financial system; address the special needs of the least developed countries, landlocked countries, and small island developing states; deal comprehensively with developing countries' debts; provide access to affordable, essential drugs in developing countries in cooperation with pharmaceutical companies; make available benefits of new technologies, especially Information and Communication Technology (ICT), in cooperation with the private sector.

Progress: Though aid to developing countries is higher than ever before, the promises made in 2005 at the Gleneagles Group of Eight (G8) Summit and other forums are yet to be fulfilled. Nevertheless, progress made has included: reduced tariffs that have benefitted the least developed countries; easing of debt burdens for developing countries, with the rate remaining below historical levels; and an expansion of access to ICT. This progress is partly due to:

- Increasing the share of world trade for developing countries
- Strengthening South–South cooperation[15]
- Transforming debt into public funds.[16]

Despite these achievements, according to the MDGs Report 2011, progress has been unsatisfactory in reaching the most vulnerable members of society. At the 2010 High-level Plenary Meeting of the General Assembly on the Millennium Development Goals, world leaders re-committed themselves to the MDGs, stressing the importance of the following areas for accelerated progress:

- Female empowerment through equal access to education, basic services, health care, economic opportunities, and decision-making
- Sustainable, inclusive, and equitable economic growth
- Renewed global partnership and a transition to environmental sustainability.[17]

Any attempt to achieve these goals requires reflection, planning, and strategic thinking. Increased understanding of the kind of work required to alter the substantial effects of poverty, leads to partnerships. Solutions to seemingly intractable widespread global problems require resources that outstrip what most governments wield on their own. They require involvement across sectors.

Not all problems require cross sector partnerships. If this were true, very little would be accomplished. The great challenges of our present and future will not change without harnessing expertise and capital beyond singular institutions and sectors. Many have arrived at this conclusion, as demonstrated in the numerous case examples discussed in this book. These forms of collaboration have been proliferating. However, cross sector partnerships are not easily implemented. They require significant attention and intentional action.

Not all partnerships are strategic, and many attempts to collaborate fail. Strategic partnerships consider the viability of their attempts, and establish clear achievable goals alongside macro long-range visions for the future. They identify the various collaborators necessary to achieve goals, and align adequate resources. As in the case of effective organizations, strategic partnerships learn from similar attempts and grow from their mistakes. They assess their progress, and maintain ongoing communication across various participants.

These partnerships come in various forms. Some focus on geographical areas, while others work across multiple borders. Some pursue highly focused short-term objectives, intending to dissolve upon the completion of clear goals. Others aim to meet long-term goals, and have no intention of ending in the foreseeable future.

Cross sector collaboration is increasingly visible. Well-known billionaires, such as Warren Buffett, Bill Gates, and Carlos Slim, have become deeply involved in high profile partnerships to address any range of social issues. Former US President Bill Clinton's Clinton Global Initiative (CGI) has become an institutionalized way to link collaborators with critical social problems around the world. It was founded in 2005 by Bill

Clinton to "inspire, connect, and empower a community of global leaders to forge solutions to the world's most pressing challenges." Its members come from the private and public sectors, as well as from civil society, and work together to share best practices and create partnerships around its four global challenges areas: Economic Empowerment, Education, Environment and Energy, and Global Health.

The CGI advises its members as each creates and implements a Commitment to Action – a plan that details concrete steps to take in addressing a global challenge. According to the CGI website, since its founding, CGI has seen more than 2,100 commitments by its members improving the lives of nearly 400 million people in more than 180 countries, totaling an estimated value of $69.2 billion.[18] At the CGI, a relationship manager with expertise in one of the four global challenges areas assists each member along the way and facilitates connections among members working on similar issues.

Further exchange and networking are made possible at CGI's Annual Meeting, held in September in New York, gathering leading figures and influential opinion makers. The Annual Meetings have been attended by more than 150 heads of state, 20 Nobel Prize laureates, hundreds of CEOs as well as heads of foundations and NGOs, leading philanthropists, and members of the media. Other meetings include: CGI America, on economic recovery and job creation in the US, and CGI University (CGI U), which convenes undergraduate and graduate students each year.

As CGI has successfully catalyzed the private sector and private wealth into partnerships with broader social goals, the World Economic Forum (WEF) has created an environment that encourages corporate leaders to partake in numerous projects. Based in Geneva, Switzerland, the WEF brings together businesses, governments, and civil society in "improving the state of the world." Incorporated as a not-for-profit foundation in 1971, its activities address: Economic Growth, Environmental Sustainability, Financial Systems, Health for All, and Social Development. The Forum provides platforms for its Members and Partners for informal exchange and interaction.

The WEF's approximately 1000 members are typically global companies with more than USD$5 billion in turnover, varying by industry and region, who are leaders in their respective industries and/or countries. Additionally, the Forum is supported by 100 "strategic partners", who help shape the Forum's projects and task forces through financial support, intellectual guidance, and in-kind services, including provision of dedicated staff to assist Forum activities. It also includes "industry partners" – companies from a range of industries, including construction, aviation, technology, tourism, food and beverage, energy, engineering and construction, and financial services.

Also involved in the WEF's comprehensive network are "global growth companies", which build global business beyond traditional markets, and "technology pioneers" involved in groundbreaking technology innovations and who have potential for a long-term impact on business and society.[19]

Through their efforts and popularity, the CGI and WEF represent the proliferation of cross sector partnerships. They demonstrate an increased interest, of the private sector in particular, in collaborating with governments and NGOs to address various social concerns. In some ways, these efforts have provided easier, coordinated avenues for corporations to participate in cross sector partnerships. Nevertheless, these partnerships remain complex.

THE IMPORTANCE OF CROSS SECTOR PARTNERSHIPS

These potentially cumbersome arrangements may alienate some people. The idea of convening representatives across government, business, and the social sector might seem far too complicated or simply inefficient. Certainly, every issue does not require such extensive engagement of multiple stakeholders. However, the magnitude of some of today's most pressing needs suggest, at the very least, the need for a new course of action. From a resource perspective alone, capital rests in various hands transcending sectors. With respect to socioeconomic issues such as those addressed by the MDGs, government has traditionally carried the burden. Across the globe, government budgets have been increasingly strained. At all levels of government, public officials have been simply forced to creatively harness complementary private resources.

The private sector relies on consumers. The wellbeing of populations impacts business and the global economy. This interdependence suggests the private sector's vested interest in addressing not only its own concerns, but also common concerns. The social sector, perhaps the most complex sector of all, is only partially defined. And, yet, it may be the most important sector given its purpose to represent the interests of civil society. Certainly, a nonprofit sector has emerged including numerous NGOs. However, incorporated organizations cannot adequately represent all of civil society. A range of other unincorporated formations from loosely organized associations to structured neighborhood associations may be among the most critical formations within the social sector.

Additionally, the social sector includes various enduring institutions, such as universities, which play a unique role in shaping societies.

Overall, cross sector partnerships are relevant to all three sectors, and some contemporary dynamics have accelerated the need to work collaboratively across sectors. Additionally, transcending boundaries for collaboration does not replace the core role of the three sectors. Their purposes are as significant as ever. The blurring of public and private boundaries periodically threatens the respective complementary roles of sectors. It is important to distinguish between strategic cross sector collaboration to address critical needs and excessive privatization which erodes the role of government. Each sector, in maintaining its valuable role, simultaneously maintains a vested interest in engaging in cross sector partnerships. This vested interest suggests the necessity to explore collaboration.

SECTOR ROLES AND VESTED INTERESTS IN PARTNERSHIPS

In some ways, the divisions between sectors are not rigid. Ideally, government, the private sector, and the social sector coexist harmoniously. Government's role is to meet the needs of the public. Its existence is supported by private resources through taxation of the citizenry. When the private sector is doing well, creating employment and economic opportunity, the citizenry is securing higher taxable incomes. Consequently, government budgets are dependent upon the wellbeing of the general public. Widespread poverty and unemployment decreases revenue to governments. Government is a public benefit collectively paid for by civil society.

Government is responsible for various critical social services. But perspectives differ widely on which public needs are primarily governments' responsibilities. Health care and education are among the many responsibilities debated. As government budgets face fiscal constraints in the context of a global economic slowdown, the parameters and limitations of government responsibilities are hotly contested. Whatever remains within government's capacity, government cannot do everything. Gaps will always remain. Cross sector partnerships fill those gaps.

In civil society, various subgroups identify specific needs and create associations. Gradually, a formal social sector with various incorporated nongovernmental organization began to take form. Today, the nonprofit sector is substantial and growing. A part of this growth stems from the various gaps in what government cannot provide. Increasingly, the private sector has become directly intertwined in government affairs. Numerous traditionally public sector responsibilities have been outsourced to private entities. This "privatization" has only further stirred the debate about the role of government. Lack of government regulation has been repeatedly identified as a driving force in the recent global economic crisis – an indictment of the notion of "smaller government". While public private partnerships can fill gaps in the public sector, how far is too far? At what point should energy toward partnerships turn toward increasing government revenue? This question will loom over all cross sector partnerships, and is the reality of the context in which partnerships are situated.

The state of government budgets and projections for the relative fiscal health of governments at all levels across the globe raise some critical questions.

Partnerships are emerging in a context characterized by scarcer resources that must be allocated to rapidly changing demographics.[20] This reality is punctuated by unprecedented challenges, including growing government debts, aging populations, and urbanization.

The OECD chart of total central government debt as a percentage of GDP demonstrates increases among the majority of its member countries in the last 20 years (between roughly 1990 and 2010, the most recent data available). In the US, government debt has risen from 41.5 percent of GDP in 1990 to 61.3 percent in 2010, while in Germany, government debt has increased from 19.7 percent in 1990 to 44.4 percent in 2010, and France has seen an increase from 29 percent in 1992 to 67.4 percent in 2010. Japan's figures are even more dramatic: 47 percent in 1990 to 183.5 percent in 2009. In the deeply troubled European economies, the pattern is unsurprisingly the same: Greece's debt has grown from 97.6 percent in 1993 to 147.8 percent in 2010, Italy from 92.8 percent in 1990 to 109 percent in 2010, Spain from 36.5 percent in 1990 to 51.7 percent in 2010, and Portugal from 51.7 percent in 1990 to 88 percent in 2010.[21]

Aging populations across the globe, especially in the industrialized world, compound pressures on government budgets. Since 1950, the aging of population has been unparalleled in human history, with the number of seniors (60 years or older) rapidly increasing while the number of the young (under 15 years) decreases. In the developed regions, the population of seniors exceeded that of the young in 1998; this historic reversal is set to take place on a global scale by 2050. The implications are serious, affecting economic growth, savings investment and consumption, labor market, pensions, as well as taxes and intergenerational transfers. Health care, housing, and migration are also affected.[22]

In addition, urbanization is also changing the landscape in which governments must try to provide for their citizens. The year 2008 marked the first time in history in which more than half of the world's population lived in urban areas. By 2030, the number is estimated to rise to nearly five billion people.[23] This unprecedented movement towards cities is creating enormous pressures on their infrastructures and social services.

Consequently, the world today faces a harsh reality: greater governmental debt, compounded by a rapidly aging population and a corresponding rise in social insurance costs but with fewer young people to pay for them. Furthermore, an unprecedented mass movement towards cities is generating added pressures on governments to adjust to these changing realities. This new landscape of the twenty-first century has indeed created an urgent need for governments around the world to turn to new and creative ways to finance and deliver public goods and services, and cross sector partnerships represent an important option.

UNDERSTANDING STRATEGIC COLLABORATION

The more contemporary manifestations of public/private collaboration tend to transcend traditional corporate social responsibility. They are grounded in interdependence. Business enters partnerships based on "enlightened self interest". Activities once considered the sole responsibility of government are now carried out by the joint efforts of corporations, governments, and a range of NGOs of various shapes and sizes, from grassroots local initiatives to large universities or hospitals.

These multifaceted collaborative structures are fraught with obstacles. These are new forms of governance, transcending boundaries typically not crossed. They require people trained in different disciplines and rooted in different cultures to work together effectively. Overall, contemporary and future social challenges can ideally benefit from combined resources across sectors. However, the process by which these resources connect and become applied toward practical solutions is inherently messy. A greater understanding of the pitfalls and potential of strategic cross sector partnerships should enhance the effectiveness of these efforts.

This reality has brought increasing attention from scholars, leaders, and policy makers. Researchers are often intrigued by the potential of partnership. Scholarship on this topic is as diverse as the manifestations of partnerships. Overall, a significant amount of the literature employs the "public private partnerships" paradigm. This book broadens this frame by stressing the significance of the social or nongovernmental sector to the cross sector construct. It is important to highlight tripartite cross sector partnerships, and recognize the potential of such endeavors as the social sector expands, and as nations historically driven by centralized governments gradually privatize.

Scholars have addressed the intricacies of partnerships' processes, as no one has quite perfected the execution of these complex formations. The elusiveness of the perfect partnership calls for continued research in this area. Moreover, a changing world creates continually altered contexts that shape the nature, scope, and potential of partnerships.

James Austin's *The Collaboration Challenge*[24] examines what was, at that time, the emerging and expanding trend of nonprofits and businesses partnering around particular social causes. During a similar period, Vaillancourt Rosenau evaluated public private partnerships in *Public-Private Policy Partnerships*,[25] assessing the value and potential of such partnerships in a range of particular policy areas. *Beyond the Campus: How Colleges and Universities form Partnerships in Their Communities*[26] was written during a similar point in the evolution of partnerships.

The development, implementation, and analysis of partnerships has matured in recent years. Public awareness about the necessity for partnerships has grown. Geddes' *Making Public Private Partnerships Work*[27] addresses the proliferation of "multi-sector partnerships". With these various collaborative initiatives, new skills and competencies are required. *The Challenge of Public Private Partnerships*[28] reflects on the accountability of partnerships, as they raise numerous financial, risk, political, and contractual implications. Overall, literature has evolved with the development of partnerships, raising important questions around the complexity of these formations.

Literature on partnerships has become more varied, focusing on segments of a very substantial arena. For example, sustainability or sustainable development has become the subject of focus in books such as *Partnerships, Governance and Sustainable Development*,[29] and *Enhancing the Effectiveness of Sustainability Partnerships*.[30] Partnerships are pursued to alleviate social challenges like climate change, and to improve the wellbeing within particular geographical places. *Public/ Private Partnerships for Local Government*[31] analyses how particular cities look to public private partnerships to increase the efficiency of government services. The role of public private partnerships in technological development has become a growing area of interest and study. *Public/Private Partnerships: Innovation Strategies and Policy Alternatives*[32] addresses the practices and policies that lead to technological change.

Some scholars assess the potential of public private partnerships for research and innovation. Spielman, Hartwich and Grebmer,[33] for example, predict that Private Public Partnerships (PPPs) created for research purposes will bring several positive consequences. PPPs provide the public sector, primarily public research institutions, with access to the latest research tools, materials and skills developed by the private sector and private companies with access to new and emerging markets in the developing world. Moreover, PPPs provide an outlet to overcome market failures created by weak property rights protections and high transaction costs.

Spielman et al. identify five possible types of research partnerships: resourcing partnerships where public research institutes receive funding from private philanthropy, contracting partnerships where the public sector contracts out research to private companies, commercialization partnerships in which private firms are tasked with commercializing knowledge into a product, frontier research partnerships where research is shared between both sectors, and sector development partnerships in which multiple networks collaborate to develop a commodity subsector. The authors found that most partnerships in their study were either resourcing or commercialization partnerships; there was little collaboration among multiple stakeholders and most often only one or a small number of private organizations were involved in the project. The partnerships did not address many of the systemic constraints associated with knowledge exchanges. They conclude that the PPPs' greatest achievement is changing the procedures and processes of the institutions such that more cooperation could be possible.

The role of cross sector partnerships in local economic development has been another area of scholarly inquiry. Christian Rogerson[34] researches how cross sector and public private partnerships may help with local economic development (LED) in South Africa. Rogerson emphasizes that the OECD declared that partnerships between the public, private and nonprofit sector are a promising way to help communities solve their local problems. While formal and nonformal partnerships have been shown to assist communities in improving their economic well-being, across South Africa there have been challenges in establishing such ties between the private and public sector. In many cases, local Chambers of Commerce have had trouble communicating with the local government and often found it difficult even to inform local officials of their existence and activity.

Rogerson identifies several challenges of cross sector partnerships, including the need to increase public awareness of the potential of partnerships to stimulate local economic activity, excess 'red tape', a need for good management of all partners, and general mistrust between the sectors. In South Africa, corruption and mistrust of government decreases the success rates of partnerships. However, many Chambers of Commerce expressed that the relationship between partners is starting to improve and that communication is more easily facilitated.

The impact of partnerships on intended beneficiaries is an increasing consideration. While many partnerships have emerged, the process of collaboration does not guarantee particular intended results. Le Ber and Branzei[35] attempt to create a theoretical framework for understanding the role of beneficiary populations to the value created by cross sector partnerships. The authors conclude that participation of the populations served by cross sector partnerships is crucial to its success. They indicate three types of power situations granted to beneficiaries – voice receiving, voice making, and voice taking. In voice receiving situations beneficiaries are not included in the decision-making process and fulfil a somewhat passive role – recipient only. In voice making situations the benefitted population receives a role in executing the initiatives of the partnership and creates value. In voice taking situations the beneficiaries of the partnership are its initiators and they take an active role in deciding upon its activities. The authors conclude that voice making can contribute the most to value creation since consent is achieved through the consistent participation of beneficiaries.

In another publication, Le Ber and Branzei[36] use four case studies of cross sector partnerships in Canadian health care to explain how partner role "recalibrations" help partnerships maintain momentum for success. They maintain that relational attachment, partner complacency, and partner disillusionment all play key roles in determining the success or failure of collaborations.

Andrews and Entwistle[37] quantitatively assess the successes of cross sector partnerships. They conclude that partnerships between public organizations increase public service effectiveness, efficiency, and equity; however, partnerships between the public and private sectors are not associated with any such increases – in fact, such partnerships often result in diminished equity and efficiency. Partnerships with the nonprofit sector do not result in any discernible pattern of improvement or worsening of service delivery.

A range of scholars have reviewed the growing extant literature on partnerships, and analysed the inception, significance, and potential of these forms of collaboration. Googins and Rochlin,[38] for example, identify four trends of the late twentieth century which gave rise to the cross sector partnership model: the failure of state economies and communism, the rise of global capitalism, the decreasing role of government, and the weakened status of the civil sector. Through a review of relevant literature, they outline the key features of the model which include: mutual gain by all parties (in financial resources, technical expertise, management capacity, manpower, etc.); and relationships between partners reinforced by "value exchanges" which are either developmental (characterized by transactional cooperation) or symbiotic (characterized by mutually dependent cooperation and exchange of ideas, resources, and efforts).

Rondinelli and London[39] identify and describe the factors which had previously impeded cross sector collaboration – mistrust, fear of loss of control, and misunderstanding of motivations and intent of partners – before categorizing and describing the different types of collaborations now emerging among the sectors: (by increasing degree of partner engagement) arm's-length relationships, interactive collaborations, and intensive management alliances. The authors then develop a set of strategic criteria by which corporate, nonprofit, and government executives can determine whether or not to pursue such partnerships. These criteria concern the specific purposes of the potential collaboration, partner selection, the development of collaboration procedures, troubleshooting, goal-setting, and partner confidentiality.

Bryson, Crosby, and Stone[40] create a framework for understanding cross sector collaboration. Based on a review of recent literature, they present 22 propositions related to the initial conditions, process dimensions, structural and governance dimensions, contingencies and constraints, outcomes, and accountability issues of collaborative efforts. Indeed, these are all critical factors determining the nature and success of partnerships.

Selsky and Parker[41] highlight promising frameworks for analysing cross sector partnerships. They identify three separate platforms for such analysis. The *Resource Dependence Platform* is based on the assumption that organizations collaborate because they lack critical competencies they cannot develop alone. The *Social Issues Platform*, on the other hand, presents partners as stakeholders of issues (and not of individual organizations); a collaborative effort is therefore defined as an arrangement of partners working together toward a single common end. The third platform, the *Societal Sector Platform*, recognize cross sectoral partnerships as an emerging trend of "intersectoral blurring" – the blurring of boundaries between societal spheres.

Additionally, they present four categories of collaboration (private nonprofit, public private, public nonprofit, and tri-sector) according to three stages of collaboration (formation, implementation, and outcomes).

The different perspectives of these scholars remain relevant. Scholars as well as practitioners are continually wondering how to increase the effectiveness of partnerships. Furthermore, as societies increasingly rely on cross sector collaboration, the dynamics of collaboration will change, scholarly inquiry changing accordingly. While scholarship on partnerships has grown and addressed a range of relevant dimensions, there is still much to understand to inform the effectiveness of partnerships. In its multiple forms, cross sector collaboration requires substantial attention to increase value. Greater value in partnerships could mean innovative and efficient government, more useful corporate engagement in social affairs, and enhanced impact from NGOs. Ultimately, greater partnership value could enhance education, health, economic opportunity, and so on.

Extensive and productive communication, capacity to work across cultural boundaries, and a disposition of mutual respect and learning are among many critical factors[42] that can improve a partnership's value. With a broader understanding of what it takes to enhance the value of cross sector partnerships, this knowledge can inform the application of these collaborative efforts. Consequently, two levels of work are required. First of all, continued research on the creation, processes, and impact of partnerships can increase an understanding of what is required to enhance effectiveness. Secondly, this enhanced awareness of the variables that shape the relative effectiveness of partnerships should help develop tools that actual cross sector partnerships can use. Indeed, a support infrastructure to bring knowledge and perspective and advise partnerships will be important to the long-term value and viability of cross sector collaboration.

This book is not an analysis of a particular partnership. It demonstrates a variety of manifestations of partnerships to illustrate how cross sector partnerships can be applied in numerous contexts. Additionally, this book draws upon the wisdom of practitioners representing various sectors who have experience of collaborating across sector. It is clear that cross sector partnerships have become entities in themselves, requiring continuous improvement similar to singular organizations. As will be discussed further in these pages, cross sector partnerships can benefit from practical tools and guidance to become more strategic and effective.

In order to understand partnerships as they can be, it is important to examine them as they are. The following chapters explore various relevant aspects of partnerships – their characteristics, value, effectiveness, and viability. It is important to review the characteristics of partnerships as they are generally currently constituted. This book's emphasis on "strategic" partnerships suggests an aspiration that perhaps belies many existing manifestations of cross sector collaboration. It is important to outline the nature and experiences of most partnerships.

The value of partnerships deserves some analysis. With partnerships' complexity, collaborative activity must be worth the effort. Why are partnerships created? In what ways can they add value? Evidently, cross sector collaborative efforts are proliferating because of some perceived value – an awareness that partnerships will achieve something beyond what could be accomplished alone. It is important to analyse this value.

And, if partnerships as they are could become more strategic and enhance their ability to add actual value, it is critical to indicate effectiveness. What are the factors that can increase partnerships' effectiveness? A greater understanding of what it takes to improve the practice and impact of partnerships is essential to the potential significance to our global future.

The viability of partnerships will determine the practicality of these efforts. If partnerships can become more strategic and effective, can they actually work? Is the notion of strategic partnerships that can demonstrably solve pressing social issues more dream than reality? The case examples captured herein provide to varying degrees some sense of what is possible. Some of them have achieved results, but most partnerships have created complex frames, having mobilized numerous stakeholders around common goals. Far fewer have made a substantial impact. It is important to believe, and hopefully know, that partnerships can become, perhaps not magic bullets, but essential vehicles to enhance livelihoods and opportunities well into our global future.

If partnerships are viable, the investment of time and resources in forming and maintaining these complex initiatives will be worth the energy. Upholding case examples of partnerships that have achieved some success can go a long way in defining how cross sector collaboration can become more strategic and useful. Ultimately, greater knowledge about how to increase the viability of these efforts can perhaps reduce the onerous time, trial, and error required to launch and execute effective partnerships.

Overall, the emergence of these new forms of collaboration constitutes a contemporary and future mega trend. Persistent and deepening economic instability in governments, massive demographic shifts, expanding health needs, sweeping environmental concerns, and many more factors all suggest the need for creative ways to leverage resources from wherever they remain. Bringing these resources together, forming structures that can sustain collaboration across disparate parties, implementing practical programs to address clear goals, and achieving progress are all essential to ensuring that this mega trend will have a lasting impact on generations to come. Greater knowledge about these efforts can play a critical role in shaping the relative value, effectiveness, viability, and impact of strategic cross sector partnerships.

Partnerships come in many forms. Understanding them requires recognizing myriad nuances and contexts. Industrial clusters have become a critical manifestation of partnerships. Indeed, partnerships are valuable in both taking on social concerns and in stimulating business and technological innovation. As partnerships continue to take form in many fashions, there is a need to take some stock of the various types of partnerships, view them in contemporary global contexts, and speculate around future directions. Is the public private frame still relevant? The third sector is an extension of the private sector in the US context, and more deeply tied to the public sector in China. Is the multi-sector context necessarily transferable? As private philanthropy grows, and the super-wealthy such as Bill Gates declare their intention to move substantial gains from private sector activity to the nonprofit sector, what will be the implications for conceptions of the three sectors and their levels of influence and priorities? Philanthropy promotes the use of private dollars for public purposes. What does this mean for expectations of the public sector? All of these contemporary dynamics require further exploration.

2. Characteristics of partnerships

Partnerships take on many forms, and employ various structural models. Some are organizations, while others are loosely arranged. Some pursue short-term goals, while others address almost intractable challenges over protracted endless time horizons. Any increased understanding of partnerships must assume diversity and complexity. If established forms of governance in nations and municipalities are multidimensional, it is not surprising that new frameworks for governance follow no single model. Partnerships are far from monolithic.

Additionally, many partnerships start with no particular template in mind. And even if they have a template, they may soon change course. These ever-evolving entities are not yet fully defined, but our understanding of how partnerships work grows. Representatives of the public, private, and nongovernmental sectors are increasingly participating in these new forms of collaboration. Participants' experiences in cross sector partnerships are essential to improving our awareness of the potential of partnerships' long-term value to society.

The perspectives of some of these practitioners experienced in cross sector partnerships are integrated into this book's exploration of the characteristics, value, effectiveness, and potential of partnerships. Focus groups solicited the thinking of various practitioners on these matters.

There is no single set of characteristics of cross sector partnerships because of the numerous different manifestations of collaboration. However, participants in partnerships, reflecting on their experiences, can idea some common characteristics. It is also important to recognize that most attempts at partnerships have not become as strategic as possible.

Strategic partnerships incorporate an understanding of the typical strengths, challenges, and pitfalls of partnerships from the outset. Strategic partnerships leverage knowledge to define their creation, progress, and impact. They take myriad factors into account early and often to establish realistic goals. Although they are designed with the mutual benefit of their participants in mind, they adapt their participants' assets and limitations. Strategic partnerships intentionally identify and select the kinds of participants appropriate to achieving intended goals.

Achieving the level of strategic partnerships is more an aspiration than a reality. We assume that if cross sector partnerships are more strategic, they will more likely solve social problems and stimulate valuable innovations. First, it is important to paint a picture of the characteristics of partnerships as they are. In so doing, it is helpful to reflect on the range of variables that influence the characteristics of partnerships. Especially influential variables shaping the nature of cross sector collaboration include:

- Scale – the size of a partnership and the magnitude of its intentions and geographical scope. Some partnerships focus on singular neighborhoods, while others address regional or global issues.
- Goals – the nature of the goals the partnership pursues. Some partnerships focus on a singular solution while others address multifaceted, complex issues with no clear single solution.
- Cultural and national context – the political and social environment in which a partnership is situated. Cultures and nations approach the idea of cross sector collaboration differently. For example, the very notion of private engagement in public matters is frowned upon by some nations. Some national governments suppress the engagement of civil society and the involvement of NGOs in public policy.
- Structure – a partnership's chosen organizational form. Some partnerships are actual incorporated organizations, while others are loosely organized, and many take paths in between.
- Leadership and level of influence – the degree of decision-making within the partnership's purview. Some partnerships have great latitude with top-level participants able to make decisions independently, while others include mid-level representatives with less decision-making flexibility.
- Number of partners involved – the range of partners included in the effort and involved in decision-making. Some partnerships actively pursue mass participation, seeking to solicit a wide range of voices, while others take a more representative approach in which a small group makes decisions. Many partnerships ultimately require a hybrid structure that enables decision-making from a small group, but with guidance from a broader group.
- Institutional backing – the degree to which partnerships are embraced by participating institutions beyond individual partnership participants. Effective partnerships, as will be addressed further in this book, are grounded in mutual benefit. Institutions (corporations, organizations, governments) involved in cross sector

partnerships can be highly bureaucratic and complex institutions that may or may not recognize how involvement in a partnership serves the institution's mission.

- Time horizons – the amount of time required to achieve required goals or the chosen time period for the life of the partnership. Different time frames can dramatically alter the experience of partnerships. Partnerships designed to achieve a goal and dissolve are distinct from partnerships pursuing longer-term agendas. Collaborative efforts with longer-term aims, for example, must continually encourage their constituents, demonstrate clear progress to motivate continuation, and often reinvent themselves.
- Urgency – the actual or perceived urgency of the issue driving the partnership. A natural disaster, for example, may create an immediacy that drives partnerships into formation and action rapidly. Perception often shapes the relative sense of urgency. Many partnerships are challenged to define or create a sense of urgency in order to initiate or revive a partnership.

Bearing these and other factors in mind, the characteristics of partnerships can vary, but practitioners agree on some core aspects that illustrate partnerships' experiences. This overview captures partnerships as they are, not as they could be. It is based on honest musings with practitioners with decades of experience collaborating across sectors. Various characteristics of partnerships and the climate that encourages cross sector collaboration are explored below.

CORE CHARACTERISTICS OF PARTNERSHIPS

Partnerships Attempt to Bring Disparate Parties Together to Achieve Ends that could not be Accomplished Independently

This very broad definition of partnerships as they are currently manifested highlights the exploratory dimension of these efforts. Collaboration across sectors is increasingly common, but participants are finding their way. Participants in partnerships generally know that something can be gained through working with others between and across sectors, but evolving and changing processes are required to clarify goals.

Ralph Smith, Senior Vice President of the Annie E. Casey Foundation, a philanthropic institution, reflected on his role in partnerships between private philanthropy and government. He said:

Because of this experience, the word partnership comes fully loaded with a set of dynamics that sometimes conceal more than it reveals ... From my own purposes of trying to develop a taxonomy that tries to unbundle partnerships ... these are intentional attempts at resource sharing or resource sharing relationships – intentional attempts at strength sharing, strength sharing relationships, and then they are often purpose driven relationships.[43]

With so many variations of partnerships, they have a common intent to share the respective strengths of participants. Participants know that they want to achieve something by leveraging their varying assets. Beyond these features, actual collaborative efforts take countless forms and paths. As they are, partnerships build relationships with the hope of sharing strengths to meet particular goals.

Swati Adarkar of the Children's Institute, said of partnerships, "... think about partnerships not just in terms of big boxes, but people moving more nimbly – not just at the leadership level, [but] how do we work vertically and horizontally when we think of partnerships."[44] In her view, partnerships are not just concepts in themselves; they are fueled by ways of working. These approaches to work suggest adaptability and fluidity.

Natalie Abatemarco of Citigroup works in the corporation's community affairs. Her work is defined by partnership. She also brings substantial experience in nonprofit organizations beyond her current position in the private sector. Abatemarco said of public private partnerships:

I have seen them at their best, and I have seen them at their worst in terms of making an impact, bringing people together from disparate backgrounds to really focus on a community issue. For Citi, partnership is really part of the strategy, both in the US and globally ... The strategy that we use is to try to bring together the needs of the community and really listen and identify what those needs are – the needs of Citi and the business and its core competencies, and then in the needs of not-for-profits, because we know we cannot affect change on our own; that we have to do it through these partnerships.[45]

Again, in Abatemarco's comments, is the general sense of the need to partner, and an exploratory approach to determining how and around which needs to collaborate. As a commercial bank, Citigroup has to engage the communities around the world in which it does business. It has to identify mutually beneficial opportunities with community organizations and local governments, but how? Abatemarco speaks of the need to "listen". Listening and communicating across potential partnerships leads to the common ground for collaboration.

While partnerships vary tremendously, some common features transcend the emergence and expansion of this collaborative trend. Leaders and institutions in all industries recognize the significance of joining forces with other entities across sectors. These potential combinations are still emerging, adapting, and defining.

Partnerships Require Significant Time, often more than Participants Initially Expect

As partnerships continue to develop, they often redefine themselves, change course, encounter obstacles, discover new issues to address, and adapt to shifting contexts. The long length of time required to make partnerships effective is increasingly acknowledged. Abatemarco said, "You can't control everything ... it does take a very long time and it is expensive. You can't just cut corners and say, 'I want results faster'. I think you really have to have a long horizon on it."[46]

Many ask if partnerships are worth the time. The time investment and expense to which Abatemarco refers discourages some from pursuing collaboration, especially across sectors. However, strategic partnerships are better able to match goals with the time and investment required. Every partnership does not have the same time horizon. Some goals require less time. But, as Abatemarco suggests, the greater the acknowledgement of what is required at the outset, the better prepared a partnership can be to meet the challenge at hand.

K.C. Burton thinks partnerships can adapt time horizons to goals. Burton is the Deputy Director of the Interfaith Center on Corporate Responsibility (ICCR). ICCR is a coalition of almost 300 member organizations that are invested in corporations through pension funds and other means. Burton maintained:

> I'm not sure that all partnerships have to be long term. I think the sense of a long-term vision is very important; but a particular partnership may in fact be formed for a very short-term kind of purpose. I think there is a distinction between operational partnerships ... and advocacy oriented partnerships whose intent is more to catalyze something, to energize something, to get something started and moving, and hope that there will be partnerships that keep it moving stage by stage.[47]

Burton makes an important point about the wider landscape of partnerships. Some of these efforts are designed to continue to advance a particular cause, continually drawing upon expertise and resources. This is "operational". In other instances, partnerships can catalyze an issue or draw enough attention to a particular matter to initiate new levels of activity. This initiation could in fact be the goal in itself. Overall, this suggests partnerships should know who they are, and know what they specifically hope to achieve. This awareness can define time horizons accordingly.

But, in implementation, many partnerships are not sure how long it will take to achieve a singular aim (or multiple ones). Chung-Lim Lee of Synergos, a nonprofit organization that facilitates cross sector partnerships around the world, indicated:

> Very often you will find that the outcomes you thought you'd achieve are not achievable in the time that you have. Meanwhile your stakeholders or your CEO are asking, 'Why are we still doing this when you said we were going to get ten percent and we haven't?' It's a challenge. I think for me … one of the largest challenges is, how do you manage the expectation of various people who have different definitions of what success will mean?[48]

Lim Lee works within Synergos's partnerships program, which brings together representatives across sectors around a particular issue that they have been addressing separately. Two partnerships facilitated by Synergos are featured in this book. Lim Lee's remarks speak to the degree of work partnerships require at the outset to establish reasonable common expectations and define viable pathways to reach goals.

Partnerships are often "Messy"

Because partners represent different institutions, sectors, backgrounds, and cultures, they must become familiar with and adapt to each other. Partners often have not worked with each other before, and so must both define common goals to pursue and learn how to collaborate to achieve these ends. Single organizations confront more than enough challenges in planning and reaching benchmarks on their own. The many moving parts in partnerships inherently elicit layers of task beyond those of single organizations. This multifaceted nature makes partnerships deeply complex, and thus, untidy or even unwieldy.

Abatemarco bluntly stated, "You know, partnerships are messy." She continued, "How do you build in the messiness?"[49] She posed a question about the challenge to participants in partnership. With awareness of the messiness of partnerships, these efforts can better prepare and adapt to the uncertainties likely to arise along the way. Essentially, partnerships take chances. They are bold creations. They create unprecedented initiatives and convene those who have little history working together. They establish goals based on theories that collaboration is the right way to solve particular problems. As with many entrepreneurial efforts, partnerships' plans encounter obstacles. Those with experience in these collaborative formations can attest to the untidiness of bringing people together across sectors around perceived common interests. The process of implementing partnerships beyond their theories and visions is seldom smooth.

Some Governments and Donors Encourage Collaboration, but Rarely Invest Accordingly

Denise Williams, Assistant Commissioner for Capacity Building at the Department of Youth and Community Development for the City of New York, reflected upon her experiences. She works within the context of a City with a Mayor, Michael Bloomberg, who represents business, and is naturally predisposed to public private partnerships. She is situated in government with responsibilities to enhance the capacity of local NGOs. She indicated, "The City encourages partnerships when we fund, ... but we don't support the development of a partner."[50]

Transcending collaborative philosophy to practice partnerships in action is a continuous challenge, and a common characteristic. Private philanthropy also tends to encourage collaboration, stressing that non-profit organizations enhance their impact by engaging in partnerships. Involvement in partnership requires time, and often additional resources. Moreover, collaborating is a competency in itself. The capabilities required to be an effective partner and the understanding of what it takes to make a collaboration work are not common. Without the support to build competency and understanding, partnerships are vulnerable. They are almost destined to fail if the capacity to partner is not thoroughly addressed.

Perceptions and Presumptions across and within Sectors Create Barriers to Effective Collaboration

In some contexts, a perceived pecking order among the sectors exacerbates power dynamics and limits mutual respect among partners. Louis Elneus, Executive Director of Haiti Lumiere de Demain, a relatively small nonprofit organization, said, "Often a large nonprofit or large owner will not deal with a small nonprofit because they think they do not have the capacity; and often these are the small nonprofits that will be able to give you the results that you want to bring about."[51] This commentary makes a couple of important points. First of all, it captures the kinds of perceptions that can limit collaboration. This sentiment is deeper across sectors. The idea that private enterprise has the right way to solve problems and the nonprofit sector does not is quite prominent. It assumes that if only nonprofit organizations operated like businesses, they would be more effective.

The second compelling aspect of Elneus' remark is the idea that many small nonprofits are the organizations that truly represent civil society. They are closer to the ground, and often bring a deeper understanding of the problem at hand. They often are able to navigate their environments and reach their representatives of their communities. When partnerships are seeking to solve social problems, their intended beneficiaries are usually represented by smaller-scale organizations or associations that may or may not be incorporated nonprofits. Consequently, when the organizations that represent intended beneficiaries are not represented, partnerships are less effective and less able to achieve their goals.

Perceptions of government's pace of operating or perceptions of the private sector's insensitivity to anything that does not advance the bottom line are also notable. Partnerships do not always surface this thinking among participants.

Partnerships do not Always Select the Right Problems to Address or Invest their Resources and Energies in the Areas that will Create Change

In order for cross sector partnerships to become strategic, they must be able to identify the problems they can adequately address or diagnose the true source of the problem they are addressing. Natural disasters often raise related questions, because they jolt people into action quickly. Cross sector partnerships are often formed to address the aftermath of disasters. However, often these partnerships mobilize substantial resources, but usually for immediate relief. While immediate relief is the essential concern at hand, it is often not the only strategy needed for the longer-term wellbeing of residents coping with disastrous environments.

Elneus remarked, "Relief must not mean just going in, put a band-aid on someone, provide them with a bottle of clean water. So, you have to look at the whole problem, right?"[52] Elneus spoke in reference to the aftermath of the 2010 earthquake in Haiti, which created a wave of donations and activity and partnership. But much of the money raised is still not spent. And the degree of devastation and death was heavily influenced by limited infrastructure. Infrastructure may not sell to the general population, but it appears to be a major area in which resources and expertise are needed.

Sometimes partnerships create new work, but do not necessarily make progress. As Williams suggested, "We have lots of activity, but no improvement."[53] On the quest to enhance partnerships' strategic value and impact, much effort is required to channel collaborative activity in the most productive possible directions.

Getting Multiple Representatives across Sectors to Work Together is Often the Greatest Accomplishment Many Partnerships can Identify

Because partnerships are complex and time consuming, and often under-funded, they often cannot achieve their desired goals. This is especially true for those with longer-range ambitions. Specialization is deeply ingrained in how people are accustomed to working. People work within their respective fields and disciplines. The public, private, and non-governmental sectors are extremely broad categories in themselves, which do not necessarily define the industries in which people work. Sometimes, mid-level employees are entering entirely new territory when they work across divisions in their workplaces. Therefore, collaborating outside of one's industry, institution, and sector is a tremendous stretch beyond most people's routines.

Consequently, cross sector partnerships embark on a colossal task when they attempt to convene participants across sector to agree upon an agenda and actually work together. The complexity of the many parts of partnerships can be so substantial that the actual desired results are seldom achieved. Many partnerships are not deterred by an inability to achieve certain longer-term results, because along the way participants become increasingly aware of the difficulty in keeping those involved interested. They are made, through experience, cognizant of the amount of communication and building of trust required. Representatives across sectors speak different languages; establishing a common discourse across partners is labor-intensive in itself.

With these many layers of effort required in establishing an effective working arrangement among diverse participants, achieving a basic level of collaboration and agreeing upon common goals is an accomplishment in itself. Many partnerships are less able than singular organizations to list quantifiable results in health outcomes or job creation. When partnerships can transcend sectors and merely stay together and remain focused and enthusiastic, they have already made great strides.

Existing Societal Power Dynamics Continue to Play out in Partnerships

Cross sector partnerships, especially those aiming to address inequities, automatically bring together parties with vastly different levels of power and influence. Consequently, some partnerships mirror these power distinctions despite egalitarian goals. Dr. Ira Harkavy, Director of the Netter Center for Community Partnerships at the University of Pennsylvania, stresses the importance of "mutually beneficial democratic partnerships". His work builds partnerships to leverage the resources of the University to improve the quality of life in Philadelphia – the city in which the University is based. He said, "The core issue for us in the successes we've had, is try as best we can to develop mutually beneficial partnerships. We emphasize very heavily the necessity for the university to be an actual partner in spite of status and wealth and power differentials."[54]

If everyone started on a level playing field, partnerships would emerge and progress far more smoothly. But, the realities of inequities pervade all collaborative pursuits. Ostensibly, partnerships assume equity across partners, and these efforts ideally at least attempt to treat participants as equals. This is a longer-range challenge for all attempts to collaborate, cross sector and otherwise.

Overall, the reality of partnerships is fraught with challenges and complexity. Nevertheless, the desire to combine expertise and resources across sectors persists. The incentives that lead to partnerships are based on perceived value to be attained by working together toward goals that transcend what participants can do on their own. This value is at the crux of partnerships' significance into the future.

3. The value of partnerships

If partnerships are perilously complex, why are they worth the time? Participants in partnerships can reflect on why they sought to collaborate across sectors. Their thinking suggests a certain necessity for partnerships – a sense of inevitability that we will all ultimately require new forms of working together in order to function.

Bill Eimicke, Director of the Picker Center at the School of International and Public Affairs at Columbia University, has held various government positions over a long career. Most recently, he was the Deputy Commissioner of the New York City Fire Department. He said of the value of partnerships:

> I don't see how you get anything important done going forward without partnerships. It's just not going to happen. As we look at unemployment in upstate New York, it is not going to be solved by government. It's not going to be solved by the private sector by itself. It's not going to be solved by the NGO sector. It needs universities, it needs businesses, it needs the government; it needs multiple levels of government.[55]

Ralph Smith stated:

> The solutions to so many of the problems lurk at the borders and at the intersection of the sectors. ... So our strategies are going to have to be inter-agency, inter-governmental, and cross sector. We have very few existing structures. Until we develop some structures, and one might contend that ... structures are now irrelevant. ... What are the networks we need to assemble that are going to be agile enough? ... we can't imagine how a single institution, any single sector, any single branch of government will be able to respond in the absence of a deep commitment and highly effective collaborative relationships.[56]

Seasoned professionals such as Eimicke and Smith have experienced numerous different attempts to address critical social issues. They conclude we must rely on some forms of cross sector partnerships. The actual structure of these collaborations is less clear to these expert practitioners. Alongside certainty of the need for working together across sectors is uncertainty about the best possible formations through which the sectors can collectively solve problems. Therefore, the value of partnerships is clear to those who have recognized the need for cross sector collaboration. But, much is to be learned about how to create and maintain effective partnerships. While many partnerships have been created and continue to emerge, these collaborative vehicles have not yet been perfected.

A sense of global interdependence seems to be another factor influencing the necessity for collaboration. Eimicke indicated on the mutual interest of participants in partnerships, "There's an interdependence – that is, they really can't do what they are trying to do alone. It's necessity; it's not choice."[57] This is true at the micro level among those involved in collaborative efforts. But it is also evident on a macro level. For example, the state of economies in Europe affects economies around the world. Industries operate in global markets. Conditions in every part of the world can shape the prospects of any company distributing globally. One single Internet is used around the world. A cure for a disease developed in one country has the potential to change health outcomes everywhere. Examples of global interdependence abound. The challenge is to create the kinds of networks and structures that harness interdependence productively toward some common public good.

The Synergos Institute has attempted to develop new formations that combine expertise and resources across sectors. John Heller of Synergos is also well aware of the interdependent context that underscores the value of collaboration. Synergos develops "inclusive partnerships" designed to address "poverty and social justice around the world." Heller declared:

> If there is a spectrum from doing something by yourself to a range of different actors from all kinds of different places working together, we're on this kind of far edge of the spectrum, with the rationale that there are some challenges, global challenges, that are so big, so complex, so difficult that government can't solve them, business can't solve them, and so forth.[58]

The role for an entity like the Synergos Institute is not to become a participant in partnerships, but to help coordinate their efforts. Heller's work is a byproduct of the growing belief in the value of cross sector collaboration. Indeed, the proliferation of partnerships will continue to spawn a wide range of approaches to increasing the effectiveness of collaborative pursuits. And effectiveness is essentially the next great challenge in the evolution of these formations. First, the acknowledgement of their value leads to the creation and expansion of partnerships; but once these efforts emerge, trial and error illuminates their complexity, and stimulates demand for greater knowledge about what it takes to enhance partnerships.

In many ways, cross sector collaboration has reached this pivotal moment. A critical mass of practitioners and observers of cross sector partnerships recognize the value of collaboration, although some partnerships have worked relatively well and others have not. At this juncture, the factors that can enhance partnerships are increasingly known, but need further clarity. In the longer run, the true value of partnerships in their implementation will rely on the successful application of what works in cross sector collaboration. If knowledge about what works does not practically inform the effective execution of the programs and initiatives of partnerships, cross sector collaboration will not reach its potential. It will not become effective or strategic.

Consequently, attention to the variables that can increase partnerships' effectiveness is critical to the future. If collaborating across sectors is essential to meeting the needs of our complex times, then the effectiveness of the partnerships that combine the strengths of public, private, and nongovernmental participants is paramount.

4. Making partnerships effective

Since partnerships as they are currently manifested face numerous challenges and require great attention and care just to stay together, it is critical to understand how partnerships can overcome traditional barriers and increase their effectiveness. Effectiveness is essential to partnerships' creation, maintenance, and results. In order for partnerships to become more effective in their processes and outcomes, participants in cross sector collaboration suggest various considerations.

First of all, if partnerships are viewed on a continuum, it is easier to understand how effort at the outset impacts the various stages in a partnership's life, and the potential to ultimately achieve intended results. In these complex arrangements, long-term effectiveness is often determined by early decisions at the formative stages. The first phase of a partnership's creation is inseparable from subsequent phases. In a continuum, causality transcends each phase of development. In other words, the steps partnership participants take in the beginning shape later steps along the way, which shape actual outcomes. Additionally, the continuum in this case is not perfectly linear. As previously noted, these efforts follow no singular formula, and encounter numerous fits and starts that further complicate the potential productivity web of actors. This "messiness" increases the significance of early stage decision-making. If awareness of complexity informs formative stages, partnerships can better prepare for obstacles encountered along the way.

RECOGNIZING COMPLEXITY

The competency to manage partnerships is based on an understanding of their true nature – their potential and pitfalls. Chong-Lim Lee of Synergos reflected on her years of trial and error in guiding partnerships. She said: "When we first started, we had almost a checklist of what we thought partnerships should look like; and what's evolved over the years is an approach that's very flexible, very adaptive, locally grounded, and relies on experience and insight that already exists on the ground."[59] She speaks of a mindset to manage expectations and take a realistic approach. Additionally, her remarks speak to certain competencies – flexibility and adaptability.

Since partnerships are complex, they can only be effective when participants recognize this reality and adapt accordingly. She suggested, "We need to acknowledge how difficult the situation is to start with."[60]

PREPARING AT THE OUTSET

The outset drives the success of the partnership. While this is usually the case, critical factors are overlooked in the early stages of partnerships. Ralph Smith suggested, "We often under attend to the amount of effort and under invest in the onboarding process – you know, the formation." He continued, "The under investment at the front end comes back to haunt you later on."[61] A great deal of effort is required in the formation of partnerships in order to shape their longer-term success.

Smith further maintained:

> So, what might appear at the front end of the partnership to be a minor disagreement, something ... we [think] we can get beyond that and put the partnership together, at a critical moment in the negotiation, at the critical moment, that one degree of error could mushroom into something that is fatal to the partnership.[62]

Agreements in the early years of partnerships have lasting impacts. As previously noted, partnerships often require a great deal of time to succeed. The required communication at the outset is a part of the reason. In considering the diversity of types of participants across three sectors alone, it is quite logical that substantial dialogue is required to forge early agreements and plans. Representatives of various sectors operate differently. They speak different languages to various degrees. And, chances are, partnership participants will come to the table with different expectations.

According to Ira Harkavy, fear of failure and blame surface in early negotiations. "When issues emerge," Harkavy maintained, "... it is important not to blame your partners." He continued, "I've been a part of failed and successful partnerships; and one of the issues that often occurs, why people are often reluctant, isn't just fear of failure, it's fear of getting blamed."[63]

SELECTING THE RIGHT PARTNERS

Partnerships' effectiveness rests on the strengths and limitations of participants. Effective partnerships recognize their true capacity and shape their goals accordingly. According to Swati Adarkar, "It's important for partners to understand the limits of their partners. In other words, different entities coming to the table have different constraints, different kinds of governing structures."[64] According to Ira Harkavy, it is critical to increase attention to who is at the table in partnerships. He wondered, "Who are your partners and who represents the partnership that you work together? You have to spend time on the 'who'."[65]

Those sitting at the table might not cover the range of experiences, resources, and expertise to address the matters at hand. While on the one hand, partnerships can shape their expectations based on who is at the table, they can proactively recruit additional participants to expand their capacity. The composition of partnerships is multifaceted, not only at the level of ensuring public, private, and nongovernmental institutions are represented. Chong-Lim Lee said:

> It's beyond having the right organizations, but it is also having the kind of diversity of people within those partner organizations, because you are working not only across the sectors and across organizations, but within organizations, making sure you have the support of senior decision makers, people on the front line who are actually going to be implementing the work, and everyone in between.[66]

Indeed, cross sector partnerships bring together complex organizations. The presence of one representative from each organization does not give a complete picture of what it means for an institution to be engaged in a collaborative effort.

The greater sum of the parts is a critical goal for partnerships: mutual understanding among diverse partners enhances effectiveness. But this requires effort. Corporate executives and government agency representatives do not automatically understand each other or typically collaborate. Casey Burton maintained:

> I don't want my banker to build my house. But I do want my banker to understand the roles that the architect plays, and the contractor plays, and the person who lays the carpet ... I want them to understand all of those roles in a way that the decisions that they have to make about being a good partner are enhanced because of that knowledge.[67]

CLARIFYING INTENTIONS AND ROLES

Clarity is another critical aspect of the context of partnerships. Natalie Abatemarco of Citigroup indicated:

I think that clarity is a key component of a very good partnership. I don't mean that everybody has to come to the table as equals, but I think that [there must be] clarity of what is trying to be achieved and ... about what the benefit or the outcome should be ... I think it is important to know the role you play in the partnership.[68]

Partnership participants come to the table for a reason. They anticipate certain benefits from their involvement. Unless those expectations are articulated and explored across the group, disappointment could set in when those intentions are not met.

Power dynamics in partnerships that can involve representatives spanning a range from corporate executives to grassroots NGOs inherently create the need for clarity. Partnerships assume equality among all participants, but this is more an aspiration than a reality. Consequently, clarity about the roles or participants and their potential benefits can go a long way in establishing realistic ground rules and expectations. Deliberate honest dialogue to clarify intentions among all partnerships at the outset can enhance the ongoing implementation. Furthermore, this candor is not only relevant in the beginning, but throughout. Because partnerships face continuous complexity and obstacles, clarity around progress or even hidden agendas among participants remains essential.

Ira Harkavy refers to "the divine right of power and wealth". This ongoing reality in partnerships combining representatives at the highest levels of society with those who are less influential creates often unspoken, awkward dynamics. Effective partnerships do not shy away from honest conversations about the meaning of power relationships in the roles of participants and the overall implementation of the effort. Harkavy continued, "To me that is a real dilemma that needs to be dealt with if we are going to make real progress in partnerships."[69] Institutions and individuals with the greatest resources, power, and influence in partnerships would have to be cognizant of power dynamics in order to actually operate as partners rather than leaders. A partnership suggests a certain degree of equality in decision-making among participants. With the recognition of the limitation of this equitable thinking in the context of real power dynamics, those with the greatest power would have to yield some influence. Harkavy said, "In these activities, if it's a real partnership, the institutions that have the greatest strength and power need to be very humble."[70] For all partners, some work is required to proceed in diverse groups rather than as singular actors. Chong-Lim Lee suggested that, in order to be effective in partnerships, participants require "some sort of opportunity for allowing partners to not think as themselves, but to think as their partners."[71]

It is also important to note that especially powerful institutional partners can leverage their influence uniquely on behalf of the partnerships. Strategic partnerships are able to use power to the wider advantage of everyone involved. In the case of Pfizer, for example, Rekha Chalasani indicated, "… maybe in the course of a particular program needing to … facilitate a meeting where Pfizer can obtain a meeting but maybe a nonprofit partner might not be able to do so … to advocate on their behalf."[72] Indeed, certain partners bring convening power – their name carries. Certain corporations or universities or governments may be able to open doors that lesser known institutions cannot.

A persistent challenge facing numerous partnerships is building the power and voice of grassroots communities. Many cross sector partnerships seeking to address social issues are ultimately intending to benefit communities that have been disadvantaged for generations. These populations have not often been heard in influential policy arenas. Ideally, cross sector partnerships would provide opportunities to expand access and influence for disadvantaged communities. Ostensibly, NGOs involved in partnerships represent this wider civil society voice, but in reality, it is difficult for any single organization to represent an entire community. John Heller reflected upon Synergos's involvement in a partnership involving Aboriginal populations in Canada in collaboration with the national government. A power dynamic surfaced in the effort by which "The Ottowan decides the programs and delivers it on down to the people … "[73] In addressing this matter, Heller and colleagues went to the community. He noted, "How do you put the power in their hands so they drive – articulate what it is they want? Put them in the driver's seat and build a partnership around that … "[74] This effort to position communities to drive partnerships is critical to establishing some sense of equitable influence.

CREATING ENABLING STRUCTURES

Once various parties join together, establish common goals, and plan to continually combine efforts to achieve those goals, some structure is required to coordinate participants and ensure progress. As previously noted, these structures take various forms, from newly incorporated NGOs to loosely organized networks. Effective partnerships recognize how to create the structural components that enable their participants, processes, and goals. These structures can navigate complex and potentially crippling challenges such as power dynamics. They can raise the issues that might be unspoken and continually pursue accountability.

According to Chalasani, accountability is best facilitated by an "honest broker". She said, "One of the things I've observed in the last many years has been, with accountability there's an honest broker who can institute the checks and balances."[75] The "honest broker" can be an outside entity or, in the case of an incorporated partnership, a staff person or persons. Because partnerships include numerous parties and moving parts, the brokering role requires a range of capabilities. John Heller maintained on the capacities of honest brokers: "It really requires a deep knowing to be able to appreciate the difference, to deal with the difference, and to capitalize on the difference."[76]

LEARNING FROM EXPERIENCE

Cross sector partnerships form to solve particular problems. They are based on a notion and are driven by a theory of change – a vision that their collaborative pursuits can improve education or health or any range of possibilities. But effective partnerships transcend theory. They envision change, but design effective programs. Their ability to implement realistic and viable programs is informed by knowledge of what works elsewhere. They tend to draw upon the experiences of their networks. Chong-Lim Lee declared:

> It's not just about bringing people together in a ring to discuss something. In the case of child nutrition, we want to see actual pilot projects on the ground – whether they are better feeding programs or better information to mothers and children around nutrition ... So, things like that – the ability of a partnership to be able to call upon its partners and tap their resources – and oftentimes it's not financial. Oftentimes it's expertise, it's connections; and to build on that kind of relationship has been one of the markers for us of an effective partnership.[77]

Greater knowledge and understanding about what it takes to enhance effectiveness in partnerships can expedite the process of launching and implementing. John Heller of Synergos said of the value of knowledge to the work at the outset, "We used to spend a lot more time on the upfront relationship building trust, and so forth ... but we've learned to move a little quicker to the action ..."[78] Ultimately, the importance of increasing awareness of the ingredients of effective partnerships is to enhance efficiency. Given Synergos's efforts to launch and facilitate partnerships around the world, a change in their methods based on knowledge is evidence of the potential impact of greater awareness. This suggests that a deeper understanding of what it takes to enhance partnerships can improve strategic thinking in the creation, process, and outcomes of cross sector collaboration.

ESTABLISHING APPROPRIATE GOALS AND MEASURING PROGRESS

Ultimately, partnerships will encounter challenges if they do not move from a broad vision to realistic goals. Ongoing effectiveness is more likely when those goals are tracked over time. Bill Eimicke added in reference to the ingredients of effective partnerships, "The one thing I would just add ... because I come from the management side of it, is developing meaningful measures that people agree upon ... and to document that you're making a difference, and that's hard."[79]

Eimicke acknowledges the difficulty in establishing and measuring goals. Transitioning from theory to realistic goals is only part of the battle. Actually progressing against those goals can be challenging. As is always the case with these collaborative efforts, the goals in themselves are complex. Some goals are quantitative and easily measurable, such as the performance of students or disease infection rates or the number of jobs. Others are qualitative, such as a sense of hope, and interest in participating, or a willingness to listen.

All partnerships are challenged to select appropriate goals. Experience suggests numerous collaborative efforts with noble goals have selected goals that address part of the problem, but not the entire issue at hand. In the context of a country like Haiti, which has endured infrastructure challenges for decades that were never addressed, an earthquake painfully highlighted the cumulative effect of insufficient buildings and roads. Much of the relief to Haiti over the years had not prioritized infrastructure or effective governance to maintain appropriate guidelines and codes. Denise Williams of the City of New York suggested in reference to malaria, "... the problem we were trying to solve with malaria – it wasn't about getting the pills to the country; it was about getting the pills to the people in the country."[80] Strategic and effective partnerships are able to diagnose problems and select goals that truly address the issue that brought participants to the table.

Moreover, partnership goals should be viewed on two levels – the outcome side and the process side. As previously noted, many partnerships indicated their greatest accomplishments along the process side – the ability to come together and break down the pre-existing silos in which participants have been working.

Indeed, the very act of coming and staying together is a critical aspect of partnerships' success. These efforts are, in effect, creating new governing structures that transcend existing boundaries that can ostensibly solve a range of problems over time. It is important to understand cross sector partnerships within the context of their structure. Consequently, their goals are not only the social or economic issues they are designed to address, but the new structures they are creating and enhancing.

These structures require flexibility and adaptability. They must build in the complexity in order to measure progress effectively over time. According to Ira Harkavy, "I do think there needs to be reflective space. I mean this is not brain surgery. It's not rocket science; it's harder than rocket science. It really is tough stuff."[81] Harkavy, in this context, emphasizes "active reflection and continuous problem-solving, and re-reflection in teams of individuals."[82] Partnerships require unique capabilities among participants themselves and as new complex structures. Partnerships must progress, reflect, and adapt accordingly.

According to Rekha Chalasani:

> It's not enough to just execute the partnership. You need to ... stand by it through the pitfalls, through the challenges, and also be able to course correct where you may have gone wrong. And I think that is ... if you have a particular goal, you may find that the process you've executed may actually set you off course to reach those goals.[83]

While dialogue and decision-making at the outset are essential to the long-term success of partnerships, there are still no guarantees that the work will evolve as everyone envisions. The goals drive the effort, but the process of implementation can take many paths.

BUILDING THE WILL WITHIN INSTITUTIONAL PARTNERS

Partnerships are effective when the institutions participating fully believe in the significance of their participation. Institutions are more likely to stay engaged in partnerships when the goals of the collaboration are in sync with their core mission. Rheka Chalasani said of her experiences in Pfizer's partnerships, "The luxury that we have at the table from an internal strength perspective is that every single one of the employees that we have working in the company truly believes that they are there because they are in some way shape or form working to improve public health."[84] Consequently, if a partnership is designed to improve public health, Pfizer's involvement is mission critical and supported throughout the company. This again speaks to the importance of matching the right partners to the issue at hand.

While partnerships remain complex and difficult to manage, our global society will still require new forms of governance that cross different sectors. If cross sector partnerships can stimulate innovations that can shape the future and solve persistent social and economic challenges, they can be extremely valuable. And if partnerships bring great value, it is important to improve our understanding of cross sector collaborative efforts in order to make them more strategic and effective. The next few chapters capture a range of specific manifestations of cross sector partnerships in different global contexts with varying goals.

PART II

Partnerships in places

5. Increasing urbanization

In 2008, the world reached a milestone: for the first time in human history, more people in the world lived in urban areas than in rural areas, making urbanization one of the defining traits of the twenty-first century. This reality brings opportunities and challenges. On one hand, cities allow for economies of scale, and create proximity enabling productivity, innovation, and a concentration of capital – all of which are indispensable for modern economic growth. Indeed, urbanization has been an inevitable rite of passage for any country that has ever achieved sustained economic growth or social development. However, when cities are not properly managed – without well-adapted policies, and plagued by weak economic growth – urbanization can lead to concentrated poverty and slum growth.[85]

The challenges of urbanization are far-reaching and destabilizing – poverty, environmental degradation, income inequalities, historical socio-economic inequalities, marginalization, as well as economic, cultural, and social exclusion. Climate change, another modern phenomenon and one of the most formidable challenges of our times, has also been intricately linked to urbanization – cities today produce a disproportionate amount of pollution,[86] while consuming roughly 75 percent of the world's resources, according to estimates by Asian Development Bank (ADB).[87] But while cities are at risk of bearing the greatest brunt of the effects of climate change, they also offer the most potential for innovation and resources to combat this challenge.[88]

Some progress against urbanization's myriad negative effects has been made to date. According to UN-HABITAT estimates, a total of approximately 227 million people in the developing world have moved out of slum conditions between 2000 and 2010. Consequently, governments have collectively surpassed the slum reduction target of MDG 7 by at least 2.2 times and ten years before the 2020 deadline.[89] Nevertheless, while the proportion of the urban population living in slums in the developing world has decreased over the past ten years, the actual number of slum dwellers in absolute terms has risen and is expected to continue increasing.[90] Indeed, magnificent effort is required to turn urbanization into a force of positive change moving forward.

Rapid urban growth has been a critical feature of the evolving twenty-first century; and it will remain significant into the future. By the year 2030, more people will live in urban than rural areas in every region of the world, including Asia and Africa, which have been the least urbanized parts of the world.[91] By 2050, roughly 86 percent of the developed world and about 67 percent of those in developing nations will live in urban areas.[92] This global trend is changing the nature of local economies as well as international dynamics, including the global competitiveness of cities.

As the globe continues to transition away from agrarian economic frameworks to a variety of knowledge- and technology-oriented industries based in cities, strategies to address some of the most pressing challenges continue to shift accordingly. These economic dynamics that have stimulated movement of activity toward cities have facilitated these tremendous population changes.

As economies increasingly center on metropolitan areas, opportunities follow. Populations seeking to improve their livelihoods follow opportunities. Consequently, urban population growth has increased, even exploded in some environments. This urban expansion has often been associated with poverty reduction, especially in emerging economies. However, these demographic shifts also exacerbate the concentration of poverty in particular segments within cities and in metropolitan regions. Certain neighborhoods known by many names (such as "slums") include critical masses of vulnerable populations. According to the UN-HABITAT, slums are inhabited by one billion people around the world – a number estimated to double in 2025.[93]

This massive population shift to urban areas and the growth of impoverished neighborhoods in cities means the sweeping priority concerns of our times, largely captured in the MDGs, are increasingly urban concerns. Consequently, strategies to address challenges such as hunger, literacy, and health must take account of the unique dimensions of urban contexts. Efforts to reduce poverty and enhance opportunity must increasingly target urban environments. The overall wellbeing of cities, with these population shifts, is interdependent with the prospects of the nations in which they are situated. Therefore, persistent and widespread urban poverty threatens stability and prosperity in general.

Nations with cities that have held substantial populations for decades have dealt with concentrated poverty for quite some time. But recent rapid population shifts throughout Asia or Latin America, for example, have created extraordinary crowding. Populations with often limited income, leaving rural areas within their nations or departing their home countries for other nations, enter metropolitan areas to seek employment or entrepreneurial opportunities. Once they arrive in cities, they can only live in areas affordable given their resources. If they cannot secure substantial income, they must remain in these areas.

These environments often include substandard housing, sometimes shanties or shacks. The experiences of these vulnerable populations in cities and metropolitan areas face a number of challenges to their health and wellbeing. Their opportunities are ultimately limited if they lack the networks to increase their access to employment or entrepreneurial possibilities. Additionally, if they lack the education and skills to secure the kind of income that could dramatically alter their circumstances, their experiences will not improve.

Strategies to address concentrated poverty have followed a variety of paths. Some primarily emphasize the geographical spaces themselves, prioritizing cleanliness and safety, and sometimes encouraging the displacement of impoverished populations. Some strategies stress improving the situations of the people residing in these areas – their educational access, health, and economic options. In some ways, this is a false dichotomy, as strategies to improve both the people and the places are important. Whatever the thrust of the approaches to change impoverished urban neighborhoods, the magnitude of the challenge cannot be handled by local governments alone. Any hopes for demonstrable change for these populations must include the public, private, and nonprofit sectors. With respect to employment, for example, it is difficult to imagine an effective strategy to provide a critical mass of jobs without cross sector cooperation. Those responsible for training must be linked to employers; and supportive public policy encourages growth in particular industries or in general. Public policy provides incentives for employers to hire at faster rates, and trainers adapt their content to industry needs. Potential employees in civil society must connect to training and employment opportunities themselves. Their access to employment can be facilitated by nonprofit organizations with an economic development mission.

Moreover, these kinds of collaborative arrangements can only succeed if they include the active involvement of the populations themselves. Because of the unique features of their circumstances, these vulnerable populations are well aware of what it would take to improve their reality. Despite this situation, many cross sector partnerships intending to increase opportunities for low-income communities do not achieve their original goals. Creating and maintaining multifaceted partnerships that can lead to demonstrable changes in the health and wellbeing of impoverished communities is highly complex. Consequently, determining how to increase the impact of partnerships is a critical concern for scholars and practitioners.

CHANGES TO US URBAN AREAS

Cities in the United States are experiencing numerous shifts. Urban areas in southern regions are expanding, while numerous northern cities, especially those with a manufacturing base, are experiencing population reductions. The racial diversity of US cities is increasing, and reshaping the culture and face of different urban environments.

"State of Metropolitan America"

In the 2010 report, "State of Metropolitan America," five "new realities" characterizing the 2000s were identified. These new phenomena, while seen across the US, were particularly pronounced in large metropolitan areas.

1 Growth and outward expansion of population
In contrast to other industrialized countries, the US maintained growth in population during the 2000s, surpassing 300 million. Between 2000 and 2009, 100 of the largest metropolitan areas grew by a combined 10.5 percent (versus 5.8 percent in the rest of the US). However, it was in the less densely populated areas (smaller counties), as opposed to cities and the high-density suburban counties, that the greatest growth took place – a growth rate of under 5 percent for cities and over three times that rate in the smaller counties.[94]

2 Racial and ethnic diversification
Since 1970, when immigrants made up less than 5 percent of US population, the figure has more than doubled, to 12 percent in 2008. Today, one-third of the US population is non-white and this segment is expected to reach majority status by 2042.[95]

3 Aging
The impact of baby boomers newly entering seniorhood on the future of health care, entitlement systems, labor market, and stock market is felt throughout the country, but large metropolitan areas are at a greater risk, experiencing a 45 percent increase in their 55–64-year-old population between 2000 and 2008, while the figure is 40 percent nationally.[96]

4 Disparate educational attainment
While higher educational attainment had propelled economic growth in the US in the past, the trend is increasingly faltering, especially in large metropolitan areas where the percentage of 35–44-year-olds holding

higher degrees stands at 31 percent, versus 21 percent of their 25–34-year-old counterparts. The disparities between the white and Asian groups versus the African-American and Hispanic groups has also been marked in large metropolitan areas: the racial/ethnic gap in bachelor's degree attainment surpassed 20 percentage points by 2008.[97]

5 Income gap and poverty

The increasing income gap seen throughout the country was also more pronounced in large metropolitan areas: by 2008, the high-wage earners outearned their low-wage counterparts by a ratio of more than five to one. Median income fell for the typical metropolitan household between 1999 and 2008, with large disparities across and within metro areas. Hardest hit were Midwestern metro areas (led by Detroit, Grand Rapids, Youngstown), with a 8.2 percent decline. Between the tenth ranked and 90th ranked metro areas, the difference in median income rose from $19,500 to $22,000. Finally, during 2008, the first year of the finance industry recession, city and suburban poverty increased, particularly in the Sun Belt areas (particularly California and Florida).[98]

The Brookings Report

In the Brookings report, "Population Growth in Metropolitan America since 1980: Putting the Volatile 2000s in Perspective" (March 2012), the following trends were identified.

After accelerated growth in the 1990s, metropolitan growth in the Sun Belt and Snow Belt slowed down during the 2000s
In line with the wider nationwide trend of slowed population growth, where the US population growth rate declined from 13.2 percent in the 1990s to 9.7 percent growth in the 2000s, metropolitan areas also experienced a slowdown in growth (though as a group metropolitan areas grew faster than the US as a whole).[99]

The years between 2000 and 2010 witnessed sharp economic shifts
During the "soft recession" years, between 2001 and 2004, fast growth concentrated in the Mountain West (Las Vegas, Boise City, Phoenix), the Southeast (Cape Coral, Orlando, Raleigh), and Texas (McAllen). Meanwhile, population shifted from high-tech centers (San Francisco, San Jose) to more affordable interior California (Riverside, Bakersfield, Stockton). Quick growth was also seen in other interior California metropolitan areas (Sacramento, Modesto, Fresno).[100]

During the "housing boom" years between 2004 and 2007, dominant growth took place in the Southeast and Mountain West metro areas. However, the mid-decade boom was not uniform throughout all the metropolitan areas: already fast-growing metro areas experienced accelerated growth, while others grew more slowly than earlier in the decade or lost residents. Austin, Charlotte, Raleigh, Provo, and Lakeland experienced substantial population growth. New Orleans suffered the largest losses as a consequence of Hurricane Katrina in 2005. Other areas that suffered losses during this time were in the Rust Belt as well as New York and Los Angeles, which pushed migrants to more affordable metro areas in the Southeast and Mountain West.[101]

With the collapse of the housing market and the severe recession between 2007 and 2010, several cities were no longer on the list of fast-growing metropolitan areas: Las Vegas, Phoenix, and Boise City (Mountain West metro areas), as well as Cape Coral, Lakeland, and Orlando (Florida metro areas). The Florida metro areas of Bradenton, Tampa, Jacksonville, and Palm Bay also experienced slow growth. Texas economy on the whole weathered the recession better than the rest of the nation; Colorado metro areas (Colorado Springs and Denver) and North Carolina metro areas (Raleigh and Charlotte) also fared relatively well, with the former experiencing a rise in growth rates and the latter maintaining their place in the top ten gainers. Metro areas such as Dallas, Denver, and Detroit had relatively stable late-decade growth patterns.[102]

Cities were outpaced in growth by suburbs in the 2000s, though both saw declines from their 1990s levels due to several factors, including:

- Slower national growth (as a result of an aging population and reduced immigration)
- Greater growth slowdown for large metropolitan areas (as opposed to small metro areas).[103]

"Large metropolitan areas" are those where populations exceed 500,000; populations below 500,000 are "small metropolitan areas".

Most of America's ten largest cities continued to grow in population in the 2000s, albeit at a slower pace than in the previous decade
Phoenix, San Antonio, and Houston grew the fastest among the top ten cities, while Los Angeles and San Jose also experienced growth. Chicago is the only exception, having lost population after an expansion in the 1990s.

In the late 2000s, there was a sharp drop in Hispanic dispersion to "new destination" metropolitan areas and suburbs
While the Hispanic population grew by 43 percent over the 2000s (totaling more than 50 million, making them the largest minority group), the eight large metro areas housing 47 percent of the Hispanic population in 2000 represented only one-third of the Hispanic population growth between 2000 and 2010.[104]

"Clean Energy Solutions for America's Cities"

In terms of key environmental initiatives in cities, according to the 2011 report of the United States Conference of Mayors, "Clean Energy Solutions for America's Cities",[105] three in four cities are expected to increase their deployment of clean energy technologies in the next five years. The top three choices among mayors for reducing energy use and carbon emissions are: LED and other efficient lighting (76 percent), low-energy building technologies (68 percent), and solar systems for electricity generation (46 percent). Economic benefits of clean energy solutions have been attributed by mayors as key drivers in their energy strategies. Moreover, for one in three cities, climate change adaptation is already an element of capital planning and/or capital improvement programs. In one-quarter of all cities, targets for use of renewable energy have been set. However, financial constraints remain the biggest challenge to efforts in energy efficiency, conservation, and renewable energy.[106]

CONCLUSION

These various trends have given rise to new strategies that tap resources and expertise across sectors. The changing dynamics of urban areas as a whole have created a context that requires creativity and innovation. Global macro population shifts which spawn mega cities with massive pockets of concentrated poverty call for new thinking and unprecedented approaches. The same is true regarding the altered terrain in urban areas of the US and other long-developed national contexts.

6.   Partnerships in US cities

The appetite for cross sector collaboration in major cities in the United States has grown in recent years. Insecure government budgets and continuous shifting of local economies and their industries have influenced new thinking about how to grapple with housing crises, the condition of schools, the need to continually improve infrastructure, carbon emissions, and any range of challenges typically confronting US cities. In recent decades, US cities have experienced varied transitions. Some have encountered population booms, while others have witnessed dramatic declines. Most have witnessed significant demographic changes.

Change has become the norm in many environments. Building an economic future in the face of volatility suggests the needs for creative strategic planning and action. Many cities have begun to look to their sources of stability. For example, in numerous metropolitan regions in the US, the most significant local employers are universities and medical centers. These "anchor" institutions are rooted in their localities. They do not (and often cannot) pack up and leave as so many private corporations have over the last several decades. Strategic thinking about stabilizing the future of US cities has begun to look toward anchor institutions like universities and hospitals to generate employment, improve schools, and address a wide range of health concerns.

Anchor institutions have created a compelling feature within the framework of cross sector partnerships. Initiatives such as the Greater University Circle Initiative in Cleveland, Ohio, have begun to reshape the local economic future. Cities like Cleveland, long characterized by a thriving manufacturing base, have declined as technology shifted the landscape and numerous industries found less expensive capital costs in other countries. These cities must build from their assets to reshape their direction.

Other cities, often in the warmer climates of the US, have experienced population expansions. Their housing markets were forced to accommodate increasing demand. However, a "housing bubble" led to steep declines in housing value, devastating the economic livelihoods of many individuals and families. US states such as California, Florida, and Nevada have been particularly impacted by changes in the housing market. In many of these economies, the condition of the housing market influences the state of employment. Persistently high unemployment has been a central concern in most major US cities in recent years.

Within the context of this range of conditions, strategies to leverage the public, private, and nonprofit sectors emerge. Since the 1970s, the US has maintained a substantial nonprofit sector. These nonprofit organizations have been financed by a range of public and private resources. Most notably, the presence of a $300 billion private philanthropic sector has infused the growth of a nonprofit industry. Funding from private individuals and institutions has been invested in nonprofit organizations to develop public goods. This cross sector dynamic has made the US uniquely intriguing with a true blurring of lines between public and private. The presence of a robust nonprofit sector, heavily financed through private donations, suggests an inherent belief that public ends can be addressed via private financing and cooperation.

The following case examples capture some examples of strategic partnerships in US cities. Within these examples, the dynamics of the nonprofit sector and the philanthropy's increasing influence are apparent.

GREATER UNIVERSITY CIRCLE INITIATIVE OF CLEVELAND

An ambitious urban revitalization plan launched in 2005 by the Cleveland Foundation, the Greater University Circle Initiative in Cleveland, Ohio, was conceived to stimulate reinvestment in the University Circle district in the city, while working towards the twin goals of physical development and neighborhood cultivation.

This effort creatively harnesses local institutional assets to revive an economy once driven by declining industries. The Cleveland Foundation plays a unique role in convening and maintaining this partnership. It leverages its position as a community foundation – a philanthropic organization with a mission to address social concerns in the Cleveland metropolitan area – enabling it to convene locally across sector. The Foundation, with an awareness of its local significance and neutrality, brought universities, hospitals, business, and local government together to jointly envision a new economy for the city, and institute a range of specific programs accordingly.

Today, the Initiative counts among the members of its coalition Case Western Reserve University, University Hospitals, The Cleveland Clinic, The Veterans Affairs Medical Center, University Circle, Inc., Neighborhood Progress, Inc., the George Gund Foundation, the Kent H. Smith

Charitable Trust, Charter One Bank, and the Greater Regional Transit Authority and the City of Cleveland. The coalition pools together investments supporting projects which benefit the entire area and could not be accomplished by a singular institution alone. These include:

1.   Housing – creating a standardized and centrally managed incentive program that provides mortgage and home-repair assistance to low- and moderate-income families
2.   Education – enhancing local school options
3.   Economic inclusion – providing job training and preferred access to jobs for qualified neighborhood residents; identifying opportunities to purchase products and services from local businesses
4.   Safety – promoting safe and secure neighborhoods.[107]

In a few years, the Greater University Circle Initiative effectively transitioned from bringing various relevant stakeholders to the table and establishing a common vision to forging a specific portfolio of initiatives. Its wide range of projects include:

1.   **University Arts and Retail District**: a $150 million project in the central core of the Greater University Circle and on the Case Western Reserve University campus aims to improve retail and housing options in the area through the construction of housing, shops, and restaurants.
2.   **Upper Chester**: a coalition of funders that include the Cleveland Foundation and the Clinic is working on a master development plan that calls for the purchase of vacant land, new retail business, and up to 400 new housing units.
3.   **West Quad**: with the aid of a $100,000 grant from the Cleveland Foundation, Case Western Reserve University is assessing the development of a major medical and technological research center in the West Quad, where Mt. Sinai Hospital was formerly located.
4.   **John Hay High School Campus**: the Cleveland Foundation, the Cleveland Metropolitan School District, and the nonprofit Park-Works are working together on $1.1 million project to create a "campus" that links John Hay High School and the Cleveland School of the Arts. Students, residents, and area workers would be able to enjoy green space and park-like settings after the completion of the project.
5.   **Transportation improvements**: three Greater University Circle transportation projects that include the relocation of an RTA Rapid

Transit station and the redesign of a previously troublesome traffic circle serving as a gateway to the area's museums.[108]

The Initiative is pursuing a compelling approach to transforming a local economy. It is building from a specific geographic section in the city, which includes a cluster of anchor institutions. These are enduring entities, unlikely to physically leave Cleveland. As other industries have come and gone, the institutions in the University Circle district have remained and grown.

The University Circle had its beginnings in the nineteenth century, when Western Reserve University and Case Institute of Technology relocated to the area, giving birth to an educational center and a new community. It grew rapidly in the twentieth century, with the establishment of Cleveland Museum of Art in 1916 and of 19 other educational and cultural institutions by the 1920s and 1930s, including the Cleveland Museum of Natural History, Cleveland Hearing and Speech, and the Cleveland Botanical Garden. With the opening of the University Hospitals in 1931 and the Cleveland Clinic in 1921, the groundwork was set for a vibrant urban district that could welcome innovation in the arts, culture, education, and health care. By 1950, University Circle hosted 34 institutions.[109]

Today, University Circle has indeed come to be known as an innovative center for health care, education, arts, and culture. The word "Greater" was added to the University Circle Initiative to include portions of the Fairfax, Wade Park-Glenville, Hough, Little Italy, and Buckeye-Shaker neighborhoods, as well as the Cleveland Clinic, the Veterans Affairs Medical Center, and others. The Initiative seeks to bring together these Cleveland neighborhoods with the city's cultural offerings in such a way as to create a competitive, pulsating urban core capable of attracting tourists, students, workers, and residents.[110]

In this case, building from one area with a concentration of institutional assets is a strategy to revive an entire city and region. This approach is simultaneously innovative and traditional. It emphasizes a strengthened local economy for the twenty-first century by leveraging longstanding institutions. The consistency of the Cleveland Clinic, Case Western Reserve University, and other institutions demonstrates a vested interest in the long-term wellbeing of Cleveland and its metropolitan area. This is a logical and creative approach to addressing the concerns confronting an older industrial city whose growth over generations targeted a manufacturing base. As this base declined, so did the city itself. If the local economy's base centers on committed anchor institutions unlikely to depart, the city's future stability could very well increase.

NEW YORK CITY HOUSING PARTNERSHIP

The New York City (NYC) Housing Partnership[111] is a not-for-profit organization developing affordable housing units in the New York City metropolitan area. The Partnership's mission is "to assist in the development, promotion, and revitalization of affordable homeownership and rental housing through an assessment of specialized programs and services that benefit the residents of New York City."[112] The Partnership serves as an intermediary between city, state, and private sector actors to facilitate the development of affordable housing that supports economic growth and revitalization of neighborhoods. The goal of the Partnership is to build 1200 housing units every year through a combination of new construction and other housing programs. The Partnership has been active for 29 years. Throughout its history it has participated in the development of more than 30,000 affordable housing units.

The NYC Housing Partnership develops projects in all five boroughs of New York City, and throughout the metropolitan region. Currently, the Partnership is developing projects in Harlem, Far Rockaway, Arvene, South Jamaica, the South Bronx, Central Brooklyn, and East New York. Most recently, the Partnership was involved in launching the rehabilitation of dilapidated properties in the Bronx, described as the "worst buildings in the Bronx."[113] The Partnership is also assisting future developments in Newark and Orange County. Most of the households served by the Partnership earn on average 80–130 percent of the area median income (AMI). However, the Partnership also manages rental programs for households with incomes as low as 50 percent of the AMI.

The Partnership's members include public agencies, lending institutions, community partners and private developers.[114] It also works with five affiliate organizations – local organizations that operate in the same scope as the Partnership. These are the Community Partnership Development Corporation (CPDC), The New York City Partnership Development Fund Company (HDFC), the Greater Newark Housing Partnership (GNHP), West Chester County, and Orange County.[115]

CPDC is a 501(c)3 corporation[116] that works to leverage private sector sources, securing public approvals for housing and working with community groups and other neighborhood revitalization initiatives. Its primary activity is the provision of no-interest pre-development loans to small developers of affordable housing in New York City. Currently, CPDC has $1.6 million to offer in loans.

HDFC is a nonprofit organization that provides title-holding services to developers during the development and rehabilitation of affordable housing developments. By holding titles to lands during these stages, the entities receive tax exemptions, which help maintain the projects' affordability. GNHP partners with the City of Newark to provide technical assistance and support for redevelopment of properties owned by the city in its most vulnerable neighborhoods. GNHP's responsibilities include managing the development process and ensuring that the projects create affordable housing.

The Partnership provides three major types of support – facilitation of affordable housing development, education services to key stakeholders, and consultation services.

Facilitation

The Partnership and its affiliates act as a conduit for numerous affordable housing initiatives. The Partnership holds titles to sites planned for development of affordable housing in the construction phase through its affiliate partnership the New York City Housing Development Fund Corporation (HDFC). This service provides the Partnership's partners with tax exemptions that help preserve the affordable nature of the project. The Partnership also assists developers secure Federal, state and local government affordable housing certifications.

The Partnership assists projects in meeting their financing needs and securing subsidies through grants it receives from the New York State Affordable Housing Corporation and through other financing mechanisms provided by state and local agencies. The Developer Loan Fund, managed by the Partnership, helps small, locally based developers and community-based nonprofit organizations with pre-development, short-term bridge and property acquisition loans. On a smaller scale, the Partnership helps its partners mitigate financing gaps. Finally, the Partnership manages a financial grant acquisition program that provides substantial funding for both organizational programs and affordable housing development.

Education

The Partnership conducts different workshops for first-time homeowners that help them maintain their new home. The comprehensive curriculum of workshops includes sessions on issues such as financial planning, mortgage qualification, debt reduction, and down-payment assistance. The staff also conducts hands-on workshops that teach basic plumbing, electricity, sheet rocking, painting, tiling, winterization, and decorative trim installation to first-time homebuyers in eight-week sessions. The new skills help homeowners maintain their properties. In addition, the Partnership provides internships to graduate students studying law and urban planning. The students are trained in the policies, procedures, and documentation review that relate to affordable housing acquisition, loan and regulatory programs.

Consultation

The Partnership provides expertise counseling and consulting services to private developers, nonprofits, industry professionals, municipalities, and colleges and universities. The Partnership reviews housing proposals on behalf of New York City to ensure that they satisfy the design require-ments of the city, that they include budget and feasibility studies, subsidy qualifications and allocations, that they implement affordability factors, and have secured seed loans. The Partnership's staff advises developers, nonprofit organizations and city agencies on the acquisition and rehabili-tation of projects in order to ensure that they will be successful as affordable housing units. The income generated from the consulting services is used to support the affordable housing initiatives and opera-tions of the Partnership. The Partnership often partners with developers to acquire and develop small distressed properties. The joint ventures rely on the Partnership's expertise in the field of affordable housing. Addition-ally, the Partnership assists developers in their marketing strategy. The Partnership arranges marketing meetings, helps produce sales brochures, and determines the eligibility of applicants.

This partnership rests within an organization. The collaboration is, in effect, a nonprofit organization with a methodology that leverages resources across sectors. In this instance, the advantage of the structure of a nonprofit organization is clear, as it institutionalizes a sustained set of activities. Not all agree that this is the best way to establish and maintain a partnership. Organizations take on their own lives and interests, beyond the interests of multiple involved partners. Nevertheless, incorporating a partnership in an organization is one way that partnerships can stabilize their efforts.

CONCLUSION

Both of these efforts – the Greater University Circle Initiative and the New York City Housing Partnership – represent collaborative structures that enable various stakeholders across sectors to focus jointly on clear goals. On a smaller scale than New York, Cleveland actually experienced quite noticeable change across numerous issues through the efforts of the Greater University Circle Initiative. The New York City Housing Partnership focuses on a particular concern of access to housing with considerable implications for the lives of lower-income residents. This seasoned effort can boast measurable progress over decades. It fills gaps in an industry that, left to merely market forces, does not provide opportunities for all of the population of the New York metropolitan area. It links the various independent actors relevant to the housing industry, who handle housing development, legal services, financing, and beyond.

Cities in the US are developing in many different ways into the future. Some cities, such as New York, are thriving economically in numerous ways, but still not able to meet the needs of all of its residents. Smaller cities, like Cleveland, which have been losing population and were dependent on older industries, are faced with innovating to develop new enterprises that can serve as future economic engines alongside the universities and hospitals that have remained committed to the area. In either instance of Cleveland or New York, cross sector partnerships can play a crucial role in providing much needed development in disadvantaged communities and stimulating innovation to strengthen the future of local economies.

7. Partnerships in Europe

The status of European economies has become the focal point of great trepidation around the world. While a part of the industrialized world, European nations are facing economic crises. Some nations, such as Germany, are better positioned to continue economic growth, while others, such as Greece, face much dimmer prospects. These nations are linked economically, despite their varied paths to development and innovation into the future. Intervention by central banks in European nations has led to fiscal austerity to weather a deep economic downturn. Nevertheless, the future of European economies will still require some degree of innovation and growth. Europe is no exception within the context of a global economic slowdown, but the deep links between European nations and the rest of the world demonstrates the extensive interdependence within the world's economy.

According to the IMF's World Economic Outlook,[117] global fiscal policy would continue to tighten in 2012, though to a slightly lesser degree than in 2011, and advanced economies would suffer the most tightening, while emerging economies would experience substantially less. Gross-debt-to-GDP ratios were predicted to rise further in Europe's many advanced economies, with G7 economies experiencing the sharpest rise. Sharper than expected slowing of growth in the euro zone in the last quarter of 2011 was due to concerns of an escalated euro area crisis: several measures were adopted in response: long-term refinancing operations (LTROs) by the European Central Bank, strengthened fiscal compact, structural reforms, fiscal consolidation, and steps to enhance the European firewall.

A gradual return to recovery is predicted through 2012–2013.[118] However, downside risk to growth and financial sector stability remains as long as underlying issues are left unresolved and an escalation of the crisis is not prevented. Indeed, unemployment across Europe is expected to continue to rise. According to the OECD, imminent issues to be addressed include: (1) rapidly marshalling funds from various sources; (2) filling in large funding gaps; (3) simultaneously addressing the needs of governments and banks; and (4) treating disturbances in secondary markets.[119]

The United Kingdom, while not linked directly to the euro zone through the euro, is not insulated from economic contraction. The UK economy grew by 0.8 percent overall in 2011 but contracted by 0.2 percent in the final quarter of the year.[120] Net exports were expected to be the main driver of growth in 2012; a temporary boost from hosting the Olympic Games was also expected.[121] While policies currently in place were designed to rebalance the economy and stabilize the financial sector, the economy has remained flat, with anticipated private demand-led growth (as opposed to public-led) not having fully materialized.[122]

Cross sector partnerships in Europe rest within this context. They are challenged to create jobs and revive economies, and address the issues that confront low-income populations and declining circumstances. The level of growth necessary to change the fortunes of these industrialized economies will have to rely on commitment across various private industries and policies favorable to innovation. The impact of economic contraction across Europe is felt palpably at the local level. It will take effective local cross sector strategies to ultimately transform European economies and societies. These partnerships can have the greatest impact in localities with significant unemployment and disadvantaged populations.

LOCAL STRATEGIC PARTNERSHIPS IN THE UK

Even before the economic downturn, certain local communities throughout the United Kingdom faced various socioeconomic challenges. In response to these conditions, Local Strategic Partnerships (LSPs) were introduced in 2000 as nonstatutory partnerships throughout the UK. These efforts were designed to bring together local councils, other public sector agencies, businesses, and voluntary and community organizations. LSPs emerged from the Local Government Act 2000, which empowered local authorities to promote the economic, social or environmental wellbeing of an area. Through the Act, the central government formalized its support for the different forms of local partnership body that local authorities had started setting up at their own initiative in the 1980s and 1990s.[123] This policy was instituted with great awareness that partnerships can harness local resources, some of which are vastly underutilized in addressing local socioeconomic needs, to collectively meet pressing needs.

These various LSPs, once constituted, have tended to: (1) prepare and implement a Sustainable Community Strategy; (2) provide strategic coordination within an area among local, regional, and sub-regional partnerships and bodies; (3) develop and deliver the Local Area Agreements (LAAs); and (4) provide support and training.[124] The "community leadership" roles that LSPs encourage local authorities to demonstrate were reinforced by the 2006 Local Government White Paper "Strong and Prosperous Communities," the Local Government and Public Involvement in Health Act 2007, and the Total Place program launched in 2009. LSPs are funded through public service budgets, partners' contributions, and central government grants.

Over the period up to 2008, LSPs in the UK became integrated in the national Neighbourhood Renewal Strategy, a cross government strategy launched in 2003 which works with local populations in the most deprived communities.[125] However, with mounting criticism of LAAs as bureaucratic and wasteful and with the dismantling of the National Performance Framework (which required local governments to meet various indicators of government priorities for local delivery), important components of LSPs began to disintegrate. The abolition of LAAs, starting in March 2011, has meant that a major aspect of LSPs' tasks has been removed.[126] Since then, councils and partner agencies have had to re-evaluate and modify their roles and tasks, often driven to cost savings and restructuring of local public services.

Despite the dissolution of the policy that stimulated the development of LSPs, these partnerships have taken on lives of their own beyond official government sponsorship. To varying degrees, these efforts have continued to progress. Three examples of LSPs that have continued are Blackburn with Darwen LSP, Lambeth First and Lewisham Strategic Partnership Summary.

Blackburn with Darwen LSP

The Blackburn with Darwen LSP is a substantial partnership, overseeing the operations of five area partnerships in the borough, situated in the North of England. The LSP is composed of eight thematic forums,[127] with a finance subgroup that distributes resources and the LAA Programmes board, which is responsible for managing funding allocated to the Local Area Agreement. The LSP board comprises 54 members from the community, local businesses, and the government; the executive board includes 24 members. The LSP is supported by a series of networks, each coordinating the activities of one sector; the Local Public Service board works with the public sector, the Community and Business Partners Limited coordinates activities of the private sector, and Community Networks works with the nonprofit sector. In addition, each of the five neighborhoods has its own multi-sector partnership that ensures the delivery of improvement activities to the neighborhoods. Their key roles include improving the quality and responsiveness of services, providing a platform for cross sector cooperation, creating a work plan, collecting performance data and disseminating the information to the LSP.

The partnership's goal is to "bend mainstream funding provided by those different organizations and services and to present a coordinated approach." Its priorities for 2008–2011 were:

1. Improving the local economy
2. Building stronger, safer communities
3. Improving educational achievement
4. Improving health and wellbeing.

The Local Area Agreement that was created in 2000 identifies seven priorities for the region, among them building a competitive economy, improving community and children safety, improving health and social wellbeing, and promoting community engagement. In the following eight years advancements took place in all priority areas. In 2008 the LAA was updated and the focus shifted to narrowing the gaps between different groups within the borough and helping young people succeed.

Improving the local economy

Economic problems that persist in the borough mostly stem from lack of employment opportunities. The employment level in Blackburn with Darwen is lower than that of both the region and of England. More people within the borough receive welfare benefits and the population overall is less skilled than in England as a whole. While wages are rising faster in the borough than in England, the gross weekly pay remains low. In addition, property prices in the area are below the average for England.

As a result of these economic challenges, the LSP is focusing on a series of goals. The effort aims to decrease the number of young people not in school or work, reduce the number of residents claiming out-of-work benefits, and increase the levels of employment in an effort to reduce the gaps between Blackburn with Darwen and its neighboring boroughs. Other goals include increasing the number of social housing units, expanding private sector investment, increasing the number of new businesses established in the borough and promoting the growth of social enterprise, thus increasing the number of jobs created. The borough also wishes to reduce poverty among older residents and increase the average earnings in the area. The borough will support business growth and technological innovation programs, as well as promote several programs to achieve its goals – public sector apprenticeships, employment agencies and more.

Building stronger and safer communities
While crime has been decreasing in the borough since 2000, the reduction rate is slower than that of the UK. A large number of assault-with-injury crimes still occur and problematic drug use remains prevalent. Community cohesion is low and residents feel that people of different backgrounds have trouble living alongside one another. In addition, while volunteering rates are increasing, they are still far below the rates of the UK as a whole. The LSP is planning enhancements in many areas that will improve the safety and strength of its community. It aims to reduce the number of victims of crime and assault, reduce the number of first-time entrants into the youth justice system and increase the number of clients engaging in drug treatments. It will increase recycling rates and improve street and environmental cleanliness.

Furthermore, the LSP wishes to reduce hospital admissions of children due to injury and reduce the number of people seriously injured or killed in car accidents. It hopes to increase the number of volunteers active in the borough, increase the number of grants issued to the social sector each year, and increase the number of LSP employees from under-represented groups. In the near future, the borough plans to create CCTV programs, establish new contracts with substance abuse service providers, promote a host of programs to increase community cohesion and develop more work for the third sector.

Improving health and wellbeing
Blackburn with Darwen residents are struggling with various health problems. Life expectancy is the seventh lowest for males and tenth lowest for females in the country. Lung cancer contributes to 17 percent of deaths among men and 15 percent of mortalities among women. High smoking rates also contribute to high circulatory disease mortality rates and other smoking-related conditions. Alcoholism is also prevalent in the borough and results in high hospital admissions. Pregnancy and concep-tion rates for under-18s are high relative to the region. Lastly, tooth decay in young children living in Blackburn with Darwen is the worst in the UK. In order to remedy the poor health of residents, the LSP has identified a series of goals.

The LSP will increase sporting activity among adults, reduce hospital entrants due to alcohol abuse, reduce the mortality gap between men and women, reduce the number of people dying from circulatory disease and cancer, reduce the number of smokers in the borough, and reduce the rates of teen pregnancy. The LSP also wishes to reduce suicide rates. It will ensure that vulnerable people will continue to live independently, improve the effectiveness of child mental health services, increase the prevalence of breastfeeding, reduce obesity among children, and reduce the presence of chlamydia among young people. The LSP will also work on improving children's dental care. Other goals listed include reducing CO_2 emissions from local government and key LSP members and reducing the number of trips to school via car, van or taxi. As part of this effort, the LSP is implementing new programs and campaigns that promote healthy living. It is developing holistic services for alcohol and substance users, and continues to support services that help smokers quit. Moreover, the LSP is implementing a robust climate change strategy to assist its members in reducing their carbon footprint.

Improving educational achievement

Since 2000, the borough has seen an improvement in its educational statistics. More pupils achieve higher scores, the equivalent of A to C grades. School performance now mirrors national performance in maintained schools. A few issues, however, continue to pose challenges in the education realm. Pakistani boys have lower achievement relative to their peers; performance in national tests remains lower than the national average; and 19-year-olds do not perform as well as other age groups. The LSP wishes to increase performance in early education, increase achievement in mathematics, English and the sciences for all levels, narrow the achievement gap, and increase the accomplishments of Pakistani boys and of children eligible for free school meals. The actions taken by the LSP include developing the Building Schools for Future program, consulting with schools and the public on how better to develop school environments and teaching methods, and implement clear progression lines to higher education for all students.

The Blackburn with Darwen Council partnered with Pennine Lancashire and five other district councils through a Multi-Area Agreement to help Pennine Lancashire. The latter has been nettling deteriorating economic conditions. The partnership's priority themes are economic and physical development, transport planning, skills and worklessness, and spatial planning and housing strategy.

Lambeth First

Lambeth First is the LSP managing the Lambeth region, a suburb of London. The Lambeth First board is responsible for all the activities in the partnership. The board is composed of council members as well as leaders from organizations across the community – the police, education institutions, health care and social services providers, etc. The LSP operates four main partnerships: the Health and Wellbeing Partnership, the Children's Trust Partnership, the Place Partnership and the Safer Lambeth Partnership. In addition, the LSP manages the Worklessness Delivery Group, catered specifically to dealing with the current unemployment crisis stemming from the global downturn.

The Safer Lambeth Partnership is a council-based team that works with borough agencies, including the police, probation, the National Health Service and youth organizations, to make the community safer. The Partnership works to reduce crime and disorder through effective leadership and response, efficient cooperation and information-sharing between different actors, and by providing accountability and transparency. The Partnership operates through a series of teams that target specific issues – anti-social behavior, community engagement, drug and alcohol, etc. Since crime remained static in the borough in 2009–10, the Partnership identified several goals for 2011: building public confidence, re-commissioning drug and alcohol treatment centers, consolidating the Young and Safe Programme, and building resilient and cohesive communities.

The Place Partnership works to improve the economic, social and environmental wellbeing of the borough. The issues that the Partnership supports are investment, structural environment, culture, housing, climate change, sustainability and transport.

In its sustainability community strategy, Lambeth announced that it will be focusing on correcting "worklessness" in the borough – a state in which people are unemployed although they wish to work. Increasing employment in the region will achieve the following outcomes:

1. Increased healthy living due to additional financial resources
2. Decreased poverty
3. Fewer people dependent on benefits
4. Greater community cohesion due to workplace interaction
5. Reduced crime through improvement to living standards
6. Greater economic activity among all members of the population
7. Better access to education and skills attainment
8. Better family support services to single parents.

Lambeth First is trying to tackle three universal issues: equality, sustainability and culture. The LSP is focusing on community cohesion and inclusion, building a strong society that is sustainable into the future, and maintaining and revitalizing the culture of all Lambeth residents. In order to achieve its greater goals, Lambeth First has envisioned seven desired outcomes and strategies to achieving them.

1. Lambeth wishes to provide a flourishing business climate by providing appropriate conditions to attract inward investment. The primary goal is to increase the number of people with access to high quality local employment. Several methods were identified to improve the business environment in Lambeth. One method is to improve the marketing and management of town centers. Other approaches include expanded services to businesses, such as improving business supports, regulating in a way that provides an equal playing field to businesses of all size, supporting and promoting innovation, and building better pathways for enterprise.

2. Lambeth wants to increase the wellbeing of households by increasing the overall level of employment. In order to achieve this goal, Lambeth First will focus on coordinated programs that bring the private, public and voluntary sectors together. Several measures that Lambeth First will take include developing employer-led skill-building programs, providing targeted advice and guidance to job seekers, and investing in a host of skills training workshops. In addition, Lambeth will promote the integration of immigrant communities into the workforce and work on removing barriers to employment within the borough.

3. Lambeth hopes to see even more children on the path to success through the provision of good quality education, training and jobs that will reduce the risk of exclusion and crime. This outcome will be achieved by pursuing a strategy that improves the physical and emotional health of children and young people, improves educational attainment for all ages, and supports vulnerable children by ensuring stable family life.

4. The LSP is expecting Lambeth to be a safe and cohesive place where people are empowered and have the confidence to play active roles in their communities. The priorities identified in order to achieve this outcome are:
    *   Cutting the crime rate in priority areas
    *   Tackling the perception of crime within the community
    *   Empowering communities to have a real stake in local decision-making
    *   Reducing the causes of community tensions that can lead to social unrest
    *   Tackling aspects of violent extremism.

    These priorities will be addressed through a series of crime and violence prevention methods. The borough plans to reduce serious and violent crime, reduce the harm caused by drug and alcohol abuse, reduce the youth reoffending rate and support the creation of cohesive and resilient communities.

5.   Lambeth is working towards improving health and wellbeing, which enables active and independent lives. The borough will achieve this outcome by pursuing several measurable tasks; the LSP will reduce health inequality, reduce premature death and increase overall life expectancy in the borough. Lambeth First will focus on prevention and staying healthy, assist people with complex medical needs in managing their long-term health conditions, and reduce mental illness.

6.   The LSP wishes to lower the levels of poverty and social exclusion in Lambeth by helping more socially excluded adults receive education, training and employment. The way to achieve this goal is by tailoring education and skill-building supports that will lead to employment and a career pathway; increasing employment for the most vulnerable families will lift more children out of poverty. Furthermore, increased employment opportunities can help young offenders move away from crime and poverty through a series of employment, education and skills-related supports.

7.   The last desired outcome identified by Lambeth is creating mixed and sustainable communities with an increased supply of new homes, improved existing dwellings and a high quality physical environment. Four crucial steps need to be taken in order to advance this goal:
   • Increasing affordable housing units and decreasing the number of those residing in temporary accommodations
   • Increasing the quality of housing in the borough
   • Improving the cleanliness and physical appearance of town centers and neighborhoods
   • Responding to climate change and air quality concerns by reducing the emission of CO_2.

Currently, Lambeth is managing several projects of interest. The Future Jobs Fund was created to help support the creation of "new and exciting jobs." Participants in the program are placed in a job for a short-term period (up to six months) in one of the LSP's partnering organizations. During that time, participants receive access to training and workshops that empower them and help them build the skills they need for their future careers. These placements help the participants – young people from the community struggling to find work – jumpstart their careers.

The Health and Wellbeing Partnership recently launched the Mental Wellbeing Programme. The Programme's goal is to "make the most of the strengths and assets of people living and working in Lambeth and the public environment [and] to create the conditions where it is possible for all to achieve their potential for wellbeing." Priority areas include reducing stigma and discrimination, improving the practices of frontline staff on issues of mental health, promoting access to artistic and creative activity, and taking action to prevent suicide and self-harm. Several actions have already been taken by the Partnership to advance the program, such as creating a handbook to measure wellbeing and running workshops on mental health awareness for community groups. The Programme is working on expanding its operations in the following ways:

- Improving public spaces and parks and providing residents with opportunities to grow their own food
- Increasing participation in the arts and promotion of local strengths
- Getting people more involved in community activities and decision-making
- Broadening volunteer opportunities.

Lewisham Strategic Partnership Summary

The Lewisham Strategic Partnership is the LSP of Lewisham, a borough of London. The organization comprises six functional partnerships and is managed by the LSP board, which operates under the auspices of the local and central government. The six partnerships are:

1. Sustainable Development Partnership, which manages issues of housing, regeneration, transportation and the environment
2. Adult Strategic Partnership, which handles health and social care
3. Economic Development and Enterprise Partnership, which works on employment, business and enterprise issues
4. Children and Young People Partnership
5. Safer Lewisham Partnership, which audits crime, disorder, anti-social behavior and drug misuse
6. The Stronger Communities Partnership, which is tasked with strengthening relationships among stakeholders within the community.

Currently, the partnership engages with multiple stakeholders from the community. They include medical institutions (Lewisham Primary Care Trust, Lewisham Hospital NHS Trust), education institutes (Goldsmiths, University of London), economic empowerment and business organizations (JobCentre Plus, South East London Chamber of Commerce), and community organizations (Voluntary Action Lewisham, Lewisham Ethnic Minority Partnership).

The LSP prepared a long-term strategic plan entitled "Shaping Their Future" in 2005, which set up the goals and activities planned for Lewisham for the following ten years. "Shaping Their Future" details the LSP's six major priorities for Lewisham:

1. "Ambitious and achieving": a place where people are inspired and supported to fulfil their potential.
2. "Safer": a place where people feel safe and live free of crime, anti-social behavior and abuse.
3. "Empowered and responsible": a place where people are actively involved in their local area and contribute to supportive communities.
4. "Clean, green and liveable": a place where people live in high quality housing and can care for and enjoy their environment.
5. "Healthy, active and enjoyable": a place where people can actively participate in maintaining and improving their health and well-being.
6. "Dynamic and prosperous": a place where people are part of vibrant communities and town centers, and are well-connected to London and beyond.

The two main principles guiding the strategic plan are reducing inequality and delivering local services efficiently, effectively and equitably.

Lewisham plans to increase access to education, training and employment opportunities, and is investing in capital projects in the local libraries and college. The plan also emphasizes adult and employment education. On safety, the LSP wishes to reduce crime in Lewisham to below the London average and to tackle anti-social behavior. To achieve this goal, Lewisham Strategic Partnership originated 18 Safer Neighbourhoods teams, one per ward, to tackle unwanted activity. The LSP aims to partner with health and social care professionals to identify and reduce drug- and alcohol-related crimes, and to incorporate technology in targeting offenders. The Love Lewisham Campaign provides an online platform for individuals to upload electronic images of graffiti and submit reports on other environmental issues in order to help improve the visual landscape of the borough. Lewisham also works to increase children's and young people's safety by implementing anti-bullying schemes and a variety of afterschool activities to reduce anti-social behavior.

Lewisham heavily encourages volunteerism and involvement in the community. The borough has over 800 volunteer organizations and 200 faith-based organizations for a population of 250,000. In addition, almost 75 percent of the citizens have participated in informal volunteering. Current programs provide platforms for young people and older citizens to discuss policy issues and become politically involved. Lewisham is planning to create forums for citizens to discuss the borough's priorities directly with local council persons.

Lewisham foresees substantial population growth over the next decade. The LSP is estimating that 11,000 new homes will be built by 2020, primarily large family homes, 50 percent of which will be affordable units. Housing standards will increase as well. In addition, recycling programs are in the process of expansion. The Clean and Green Schools program teaches children about their role in protecting the environment. The borough plans on offering its citizens the opportunity to choose their energy providers, which will include alternative energy. Additional environmentally-friendly initiatives will be adopted – green and clean parks, green roofing, and better waterways to reduce flooding damage.

In order to improve the health of residents, "Shaping Their Future" identifies several goals focusing on achieving a healthier lifestyle. New sports and leisure facilities have been opened, and the LSP is leading new initiatives that promote healthy lives for older people, like the Healthy Walks and Everyday Swim programs. The plan is also looking to improve the health of young people and children by fighting child obesity through the MEND program and screening teens aged 15–24 for chlamydia. Additional goals for improving the health of Lewisham citizens were identified in "Shaping Their Future": supporting people who wish to stop smoking, providing health services closer to people's homes, and providing assistance to long-term care patients through public agencies and voluntary organizations, community schemes to reduce isolation and schools that provide services to children with disabilities.

The 2020 plan sets up goals for improving the economic prosperity of the borough. Collaboration is already taking place between town center managers and local business owners, and the Creative Lewisham Agency supports the creative enterprises in the borough. There are several developments and extensions of town centers and main streets planned for the next few years. In addition, the partnership plans to offer expanded education and skills training for workers and to promote business clustering. Transportation will also be improved, including both public and private transportation. The London Cycle Network Plus has been completed, providing bicycle routes across the capital. Lastly, Lewisham is working to ensure that transportation is accessible to all residents.

All three of these examples of LSPs represent comprehensive initiatives addressing the priority matters facing populations within particular boroughs. Each partnership is a new structure – an unprecedented multi-stakeholder creative form of governance. The role of governments in boroughs, through these partnerships, is transformed to catalyze collaboration across the various institutions within their boundaries. It took national-level policy to spawn their partnerships, but local commitment will be required to maintain the effort and programming established to date. These collaborative structures have ushered in new and deeper degrees of interaction across participating institutions. By leveraging institutional partnerships through local governments, the LAAs developed potentially permanent formations. Since the partnerships are extensions of government, they represent innovative forms of public management.

The LSPs' effort represented extensive national policy in the United Kingdom. This monumental effort encouraged cross sector cooperation as a means to address critical challenges confronting municipalities and neighborhoods. Becoming integrated into national policy would be a goal for many cross sector partnerships. In this instance, policy was not only an achievement; it was the driver. However, this mandate and opportunity still did not lead to longer-term sustainability in the face of changing political administrations and an economic downturn. Looking forward, many of the collaborative structures that have chosen to remain in place despite changed policies must continually consider how they will sustain their efforts. All of these partnerships raise important questions about the long-term viability of partnerships after they are created, and in this case, supported by public policy.

STRATEGIC PARTNERSHIPS IN GERMANY

AutoVision

Throughout Europe, strategies for economic development are paramount. These approaches are inherently cross sector, as they require cooperation between government and business. Economic clusters have been one way in which various local areas have aligned public sector commitments with planned industry growth. Government incentives can offer certain industries growth opportunities. AutoVision is one example of an economic cluster with the auto industry in Germany.

In 1998, Volkswagen (VW), in partnership with the northern German city of Wolfsburg, set out on an ambitious project: creating an economic cluster in Wolfsburg that would pool companies and related institutions focused on a specific technological area, in an automotive cluster.[128] The project, "AutoVision," sought to attract high-tech start-ups, suppliers, and other companies relevant to the automotive industry to the city. The idea of such economic clusters was not new. The most illustrious examples of these are well known: the film industry in Hollywood, the high-tech industry in Silicon Valley, or the toy industry in Nuremberg.

AutoVision was an effort to revive Wolfsburg, a city with under 130,000 inhabitants and home to VW's headquarters and main plants. The city had once been a boom town when the VW Beetle represented Germany's rapid economic growth during the 1950s, with around 70,000 workers employed at one of its VW plants in the 1980s at its peak. But as a crisis enveloped the automotive industry in 1992, VW in Wolfsburg was hit hard: some 15,000 workers saw their jobs disappear within a few years and those remaining saw their working hours significantly reduced.[129]

When local unemployment reached 19 percent in 1998, VW decided to take action. It enlisted the help of McKinsey & Company to develop a plan to create a self-sustaining business environment – an economic cluster – in Wolfsburg. In 1999, VW and the city of Wolfsburg jointly founded the Wolfsburg AG to manage the cluster-building initiatives that the AutoVision project required.

The project set out to cut local unemployment in half by 2003. It sought to foster a mobility cluster focused on VW, linking it to other industries (namely the ICT, leisure industry, and health care services). The program established the Innovation Campus that nurtures start-up ventures (a process known as "tech-farming") and holds an annual nationwide business-plan competition to lure these ventures to the city. The Supplier Location Services was also established, allowing suppliers' engineers to work directly with their VW counterparts in the development of new cars and components in the simultaneous-engineering center. Another important initiative has been the *ErlebnisWelt*, which seeks to turn Wolfsburg, previously lacking in tourist appeal, into a desirable destination by offering a new range of leisure and entertainment facilities around the Autostadt, an automotive theme park showcasing VW's brands. The Autostadt, with around 2000 staff, now attracts some two million visitors to Wolfsburg each year. Additionally, AutoVision created a human resources agency to facilitate the allocation of jobs created by

AutoVision to the local labor force. This agency provides services ranging from recruiting, temporary staffing, outplacement, personnel consulting, and qualification and training measures.[130]

As a result of these efforts, over 240 new businesses were formed by 2005, and more than 100 suppliers had relocated to the area, resulting in 23,000 jobs. Since 2005, Wolfsburg has also hosted one of the largest automotive suppliers' trade fairs in Europe, the *Internationale Zuliefererbörse*.[131] The project is not without its critics, who point out the dangers of excessive dependency of the local economy on the fate not of only one industry, but of one company. Yet, the city is without many other viable alternatives. At play here, then, is a delicate balancing act between promoting growth and competitiveness of a city and the stability of regional policy.[132]

Renewable Energy Hamburg

Renewable Energy Hamburg is another example of a business cluster that strengthens and promotes cooperation in the renewable energy industry in the City of Hamburg and the neighboring metropolitan area.[133] The cluster aims to secure and promote the positive outcomes of renewable energy – increased quality of life, environmental protection and economic development – for the long term. The success of the renewable energy industry is primarily dependent on exports. The Renewable Energy Hamburg cluster has more than 140 members in its network, rising from 57 members at the time of launch in September 2010.

The renewable energy industry is a major force in the Hamburg region. Several hundred companies and service providers are active in the industry in the region, and the largest 25 renewable energy companies employ almost 4,000 locals.[134] The cluster's members include a wide range of companies, research institutions and other regenerative energy industry institutions. The cluster's shareholders are the Free and Hanseatic City of Hamburg, which owns 51 percent of the shares, and the Association for the Promotion of the Renewable Energy Cluster (the Association), which owns 49 percent of the shares.[135]

The Association for the Promotion of the Renewable Energy Cluster was founded on September 29, 2010, and it serves as manager and administrator of the cluster. The Association provides linkages between companies, universities, other relevant institutions, and the public sector. Its goal is to develop and strengthen sustainability in the region, which it promotes through cross-industry synergies. The Association facilitates the operations of several working groups that focus on different components of the renewable energy industry.

1. **Research and Development Working Group**: this group acts as an interface between application and research by providing a platform in which experts share their views and discuss new developments in the industry.
2. **Media and Renewable Energies Working Group**: this group brings together communications experts and officers from renewable energy companies to share ideas and strengthen the message of renewable energies. By using examples of best practices, companies can develop joint media public relations strategies for the cluster and the metropolitan area.
3. **Financial and Legal Services Working Group**: this group provides networks for financial, legal and insurance experts to discuss issues and problems pertaining to renewable energies in order to draw up solution proposals. The working group also designs standards and guidelines that help strengthen the industry center.
4. **Personnel and Qualification Working Group**: this group meets to discuss solution strategies for fulfilling future personnel needs. The working group also evaluates the effectiveness of short-term measures such as additional education, qualification and recruitment.

The Association publishes a newsletter that reports on the business cluster. The first newsletter was published in October 2011. Highlights from the newsletter include:

- The Berufsakademie Hamburg is now offering a bachelor's degree course in Technology and Management Renewable Energies and Energy Efficiency as a result of the growth in energy industry activity in the region. The course-of-study targets electronic technicians in energy and building services, plant mechanics and roofers. The degree program combines on-the-job training and academic studies in management or technology.
- Representatives from the Estonian Wind Power Association visited Erneuerbare Energien Hamburg to attract German costumers. The Association has about 30 national and international members.
- The Renewable Energy Hamburg Cluster joined the International Cleantech Network (ICN) – a network between the world's leading clean technology cluster organizations. ICN holds joint transnational events to network with member companies from all the networks in order to facilitate knowledge-sharing.

The cluster continues to grow and influence the renewable energy sector in Hamburg. "In the future the Hamburg Renewable Energies Cluster will advocate even greater networking among existing companies in the industry and the promotion of new ideas, project corporations and start-ups."[136]

These economic clusters strategically align policy, particular industries, and educational/training institutions. They can deepen the commitment of industries to particular localities and stimulate substantial job opportunities. They may not address the comprehensive range of challenges facing European nations, but their ability to increase employment and build marketable skills for residents can certainly help address critical socio-economic needs. Selecting the right industry is a part of the challenge. Within the context of a dynamic, constantly changing, global economy, it will be important to identify industries with growth opportunities into the future.

SLOVAKIA CROSS SECTOR COOPERATION (CSC)

Variation across Europe may influence the differential prospects of nations. While public private partnerships may have taken root in Germany and the UK, cross sector partnerships in Slovakia are not very developed. In this context, one would find a weak culture of corporate philanthropy and little respect for the law, which might serve as deterrents to strengthened relationships between the public, private and nonprofit sectors in Slovakia.

In order to promote cooperation among sectors and to boost Slovakia's reputation as its accession to the European Union was approaching (2004), the Slovakian government implemented legal changes to stimulate CSC and create sustainable partnerships. The most influential initiative was a change in the tax structure that allows businesses to contribute up to 2 percent of their income tax to NGOs. In order to assess how the legal changes might assist in promoting CSC, the Trust for Civil Society in Central and Eastern Europe, a public charity focused on the development of civil society in the region, conducted an analysis of the state of partnerships in Slovakia from 2002 to 2005.[137] The analysis provides great insight into the particular challenges of partnerships in emerging markets that stem from a weak culture of philanthropy and volunteerism.

Slovakia became an independent state in 1993 after the break-up of Czechoslovakia. Since 1993 Slovakia has made great economic and social strides, which include reforms in the country's tax code and health care, pension and social welfare system.[138] However, economic growth stagnated after 2000.[139] Many efforts leading to the country's accession to the EU focused on sustainable economic development. Promoting partnerships between the public, private, and nongovernmental sectors was included in the plans to achieving the country's development goals.

As a result, the Trust for Civil Society in Central and Eastern Europe improved the environment in which NGOs operated its priority for 2002–2005. In Slovakia the Trust established a local program to improve conditions for cooperation between the three sectors. One of the goals of the program was to identify industry needs and recommend improvements. The program included comprehensive research of the cooperation potential between the sectors, which included surveys and focus groups. The findings of the research and recommendations for improving the environment for sustaining cross sector partnerships in Slovakia are described below.

CSC before the Reform

Slovakia has experienced limited CSC in recent years on a national level. However, collaboration across the sectors has been more frequently pursued on the regional level. In surveys, many noted that cross sector collaboration has been intensifying and that partnerships are increasingly integrated into regional development strategies.

Most of the cooperation between the private and nonprofit sectors occurs through one-time corporate donations. The private sector provides financing for community development by donating to community foundations, funds and other organizations. However, no single private foundation focuses on the development and support of cross sector collaboration.

Few partnerships are long-term strategic partnerships. As a result of government reforms and the decentralization of government, cooperation between the public and nongovernmental sector is increasing. The integration of Slovakia into the EU has also been a driving force for cooperation between the two sectors. Slovakia has no defined model for organizing and financing cross sector partnerships, which might result in the development of a new collaborative model in Slovakia. Partners do not communicate with each other regularly. The lack of brand recognition of NGOs hinders the success of cross sector collaboration in Slovakia, as they are characterized as unprofessional, poor communicators and presenters with bad reputations.

The authors of the study identified basic roadblocks in the Slovakian legal system to building cross sector partnerships. First, there are few legal differences between the private and nongovernmental sectors. This results in constant intervention between the sectors, for example through state-owned enterprises. In addition, the nongovernmental legal structure is less developed compared with business law, and is insufficient to provide the support needed for the sector. Legislation of the third sector will need to clearly define the types of organizations that fall under the category of NGOs, create a registration system for nonprofits, and update legislation that regulates charitable giving in the country.

The lack of information regarding the activities of NGOs can be remedied through creating registers and databases. It is also important that partners are correctly chosen so that they can provide the best services for the partnership. The involvement of the business community is often very helpful. Partners need to show respect to one another and see the value of participating in the partnership for it to succeed.

Two Percent Corporate Income Tax Allocation

Since 2004 all businesses in Slovakia can choose to allocate 2 percent of their income tax towards registered NGOs.[140] The financing is provided for public purposes through tax returns, and can be anonymous. The corporate tax mechanism has had a significant impact on cooperation between businesses and NGOs.[141] In 2004, 92.71 percent of the entire possible tax allocation was in fact paid to NGOs. By 2007, approximately €29.3 million have been provided to NGOs through this mechanism.[142] The success of the tax allocation is unequivocal and has great potential to improve the state of cross sector partnerships in Slovakia.

Representatives of mid-size companies view the tax mechanism positively. They are motivated to participate in this scheme because they want to help and support concrete social programs. Many firms stated that they see more potential for NGOs to receive greater financial means through the mechanism than if they relied on government budget decisions alone. The NGOs that received support were chosen by the companies themselves, mostly based on a formal request made by the nonprofits and through a personal connection between the organizations and the companies. NGOs that were conducting activities of interest to specific companies or that benefitted the company had a greater chance of receiving funding. Additional factors that contributed to the distribution of funds to an NGO were the reputation of the organization and whether it implemented controls to its financial management. The fields that received the majority of the funding were health, sports, education and research, and children and youth.

Many businesses do not expect to receive any benefit from participating in the scheme. Few organizations expressed any interest in promoting their 2 percent tax donation. The media too does not take an active role in promoting funding provided to the nongovernmental sector by the private sector, which creates tension between the media and businesses. At the same time, most firms view the 2 percent income tax allocation mechanism as corporate philanthropy, although the companies would have paid the amount in taxes otherwise.

Overall, there are signs that cross sector collaboration and the potential for future long-lasting partnerships is improving. While the effect of the 2 percent income tax mechanism is unknown and it is still unclear whether it will result in the crowding out of other forms of corporate philanthropy, the institutions surveyed expressed optimism regarding collaboration in the future. Slovakia will have to work harder to promote cross sector partnerships in the next several years as it develops economically and become less dependent on EU funds.

CONCLUSION

It is interesting that a critical feature in encouraging cross sector collaboration in Slovakia has been changing the tax code. Indeed, the civic/nongovernmental sector is essential to enabling the involvement of civil society in collaborative efforts to address priority concerns. Leveraging the tax code to develop a nongovernmental sector is an important proven strategy to increase the size and influence of organizations that represent civil society. The Slovakian experience reminds us of the importance of preconditions for cross sector partnerships. Contexts conducive to collaboration across sectors require a certain level of infrastructure and public will. In the UK and Germany, partnerships were created from starting points that are more favorable than those in Slovakia.

Overall, the economic crisis in Europe can create the kind of urgency that can accelerate action, and crystallize the potential value in working together beyond sector boundaries. Economic and community development partnerships in localities with supportive national policy could prove essential for the future of Europe.

8. Partnerships in emerging markets

Today, emerging nations are exerting an increasingly large influence in the world economy. As of 2006 (before South Africa's inclusion), BRIC (Brazil, Russia, India, and China) countries accounted for 40 percent of the world's population and nearly 25 percent of global GDP. In projections made in 2006, India's economy is expected to be larger than Japan's by 2032, and China's larger than the US by 2041. As a whole, the BRIC economies could be larger than that of the G6 by as early as 2039.[143] They proved more resistant to the 2008–9 global crisis than the advanced economies and were key players in the economic recovery, although this seeming immunity has changed more recently. Five of the top 20 companies in the 2010 Forbes Global 2000 list come from the BRIC countries (three from China, one from Russia, and one from Brazil).[144]

BRAZIL

According to the "OECD Economic Surveys – Brazil (October 2011)," Brazil has made notable economic, social, and environmental progress since the mid-1990s, which has driven robust growth and has allowed it to compete with high-income countries. These progresses have been namely:

- Economic and financial stability, increased resilience – due in large part to the strengthening of public institutions (inflation-targeting framework, exchange rate flexibility, and the Fiscal Responsibility Law in particular)
- Decreased poverty and inequality
- Improved environmental sustainability.

Brazil has experienced a steady appreciation of its currency since 2003, with certain exceptions, as during the 2008 financial crisis. It marked its highest annual growth since 1986 in 2010 (7.5 percent in real GDP growth), ranking it the fifth best performer among the G20 countries. Over the next two years (from October 2011), real GDP growth is predicted to slow less than 4 percent (below the 4.5 percent per year trend rates), while inflation is projected to diminish gradually but remain in the upper part of 2.5–6.5 percent, which is the target range.[145] The OECD survey calls for the fostering of productive investment, particularly infrastructure development, in order to boost output growth and reduce poverty. Social and education policies have been identified as having the potential to raise long-term income gains by upgrading skills. The steady increase of oil production since 2003 plus the discovery of large quantities of offshore oil reserves will make Brazil one of the top ten countries for oil reserves.

However, Brazil's aging population – in less than 20 years the elderly population is expected to double – will change the economic context. It will, for example, put the country at risk for lower output growth by the middle of the century, though the Growth Acceleration Programme (PAC) is expected to partially compensate for the fall in productivity.[146]

RUSSIA

According to the "OECD Economic Surveys – Russian Federation (December 2011)," Russia is recovering from the severe 2008–9 recession, though it is not yet back at its pre-crisis activity levels. It also faces relatively high inflation, albeit declining. Recent years have seen an emphasis on modernizing the economy, with reduced dependence on oil revenues and a diversified economy. Efforts have been made especially in view of accession to the OECD. Russia also enjoys relatively flexible markets.[147] The population is well educated, with exceptionally high rates of tertiary enrolment.[148] It has a negative net public debit (public financial assets exceed gross public debt), thanks to prudent policies that saved much of the oil price windfalls over the past decade and relatively advanced budgeting procedures.[149] Since the global crisis, the Central Bank of Russia has also announced its intention for a new framework for monetary policy in order to move towards an inflation-targeting regime.

However, Russia faces a complex business environment, characterized by pervasive state involvement in the economy, widespread corruption, weak rule of law, and relatively restrictive foreign trade and investment regimes. These dynamics have led to low levels of competition, weak innovation, low investment, and greater dependence on natural resource extraction. Furthermore, insufficient energy efficiency efforts have greatly contributed to poor environmental outcomes and to its high-carbon economy.[150]

CHINA

According to OECD's "China in Focus: Lessons and Challenges" (2012), China is now ranked as an upper middle-income country with a GDP per capita nearing some advanced economies. Chinese GDP has almost tripled in size since 2000, with an annual growth rate of over 9 percent in consecutive years. However, at 9.2 percent in 2011, the Chinese economy experienced one of its slowest expansions in a decade, though the figure is still high by global standards.[151] But the slowing of economy (with just above 8 percent growth by the end of 2011) is the result of its efforts to cool the economy and reduce inflation. Inflationary pressures have prompted tightening of monetary policy.

In 2012, real GDP growth is expected to remain below 9 percent but to pick up later in the year and into 2013 with improvements in the global economy.[152] In common with advanced economies, two of China's major challenges are inequality and environmental sustainability.[153]

Furthermore, according to the CIA World Factbook,[154] coastal provinces have experienced more economic development than the interior, and more than 250 million migrant workers and their dependants had relocated to urban areas to work by 2011. Today, China's population control policy has meant that it now has one of the most rapidly aging populations in the world.

The CIA identified the economic challenges faced by the Chinese government as the following:

● Reducing its high domestic savings rate and low domestic demand
● Sustaining adequate job growth for tens of millions of migrants and new entrants to the workforce
● Reducing corruption and other economic crimes
● Containing environmental damage and social unrest resulting from the economy's rapid growth.

INDIA

According to the "OECD Economic Surveys – India (June 2011)," India has made great strides in development, though the productivity gap with OECD countries remains large. Its share of global output has continued to rise and income per capita doubled in just over 11 years, since 1990.[155] Private investment has been a key driving force in the growth, supported by strong corporate sector profitability and increasing national saving rate.

Prior to the global recession, annual growth was over 9 percent (the highest in Indian history), which exceeded the already high growth rates of the early 2000s.[156] India also demonstrated resilience to the global crisis: it was one of the first economies to recover, thanks to strong domestic demand, and most of its banks were deemed able to meet Basel III regulations, with only a small number of state-owned banks needing capital injections.[157]

India's poverty rate has fallen, but it remains high given its strong growth (though the introduction of the national rural employment guarantee has helped make growth more inclusive). India's health spending, as a percent of GDP, is one of the lowest in the world – only seven other governments spend less on health. The result is poor public health and exacerbated poverty. Furthermore, despite efforts to improve educational access and quality – for example the Right to Education Act 2009, which is helping to accelerate efforts for universal elementary education – problems of high drop-out rates, low student attendance, and teacher absence persist.[158] Lastly, renewed reforms that promote investment are necessary for even faster growth.[159]

SOUTH AFRICA

According to the CIA World Factbook, South Africa is a middle-income, emerging market with an abundant supply of natural resources. Its financial, legal, communications, energy, and transport sectors are well developed, and its stock exchange ranks eighteenth in the world in terms of size. Between 2004 and 2007, South Africa experienced robust growth, which began to slow in the second half of 2007 after an electricity crisis and the global financial crisis. Unemployment is high and growth has been constrained by outdated infrastructure. South Africa also suffers from the aftermath of the apartheid era, in particular poverty, weak economic empowerment among the disadvantaged groups, and lack of public transportation.[160]

South Africa's growth path has been largely led by domestic demand in recent years. Its characteristics include: low savings and investment rates, weak export performance, overvalued currency, and high unemployment. The global recession hit South Africa after it had passed its boom years, and the economy experienced a sharp slowdown and its first recession in 17 years. However, the banks did not experience a crisis and growth has resumed. But to boost growth, the OECD recommends better use of its favorable endowments (labor and natural resources).[161]

EMERGING ECONOMIES AND THE NORTH/SOUTH DIVIDE

The Brandt Reports, published in 1980 by the Independent Commission on International Development Issues and led by the former Chancellor of West Germany, Willy Brandt, highlighted the socioeconomic divide between wealthier nations in the Northern Hemisphere and developing nations in the Southern Hemisphere. The Brandt Reports recommended a comprehensive restructuring of the global economy and new ways to address international development. In 2001, an updated version, "The Brandt Equation – 21st Century Blueprint for the New Global Economy," by James Quilligan, was published. According to this updated report, "Two decades later, the international community has not responded to these proposals in any meaningful way … the economic disparities outlined in the Brandt Reports have widened significantly since 1980."[162] However, while the international community still has a long way to go, some encouraging results have also been produced: for example, according to the World Bank, within the developing world, those living under the international poverty line of $1.25 a day has reduced from 1.9 billion people in 1990 to 1.29 billion in 2008, or 43 percent of the population in 1990 to 22.4 percent in 2008.[163]

Nonetheless, the Brandt Reports highlighted several fundamental factors undermining development in the Southern Hemisphere, as distinct from those in the Northern Hemisphere:

1. **Poverty**: whereas in the North, poverty is created by the unequal distribution of wealth, the South faces the problem of lack of resources to begin with and the paucity of opportunities to acquire wealth.
2. **Health**: while the South has seen an increase in life expectancy, malnutrition as well as lack of access to medical care, safe water, and sanitation continue to plague the developing world.
3. **Housing**: the combination of urbanization, high birth rates, unemployment, and poverty have created the reality that even the cheapest housing eludes up to two-thirds of families in certain cities in developing countries.
4. **Education**: the enrolment of girls in schools is significantly low, even while progress has been made in the numbers attending school in developing countries.

5.   **Women**: the role of women in development is emphasized and calls for the education and employment of women in any developmental project.[164]

Moreover, according to Branko Milanovic, lead economist at the World Bank and a leading expert on inequality, 80 percent of one's likely income is determined at birth by citizenship and family income class. He argues that even if mobility within one's country may be possible with enough hard work and luck, it is nonetheless much harder to improve one's ranking on a global scale, unless one's country itself grows,[165] and this is why high growth in poor countries is highly significant. This reality of global inequality makes it ever harder for those in the South to transition out of the vicious circle of poverty, and deepens the North–South divide.

Furthermore, climate change has exacerbated the North–South divide. Battling climate change requires a global collective action, but the prospect of having to make difficult adjustments raises endless tensions between the developed countries, the bulk of whom are taking the lead in putting pressure to make international agreements on climate change mitigation, and the developing countries, who feel unfairly burdened. For the countries of the South, it feels less pertinent to clean up what rich countries created, especially when they are struggling with the fundamental challenge of pulling their countries out of poverty. Moreover, developed countries' green technological advancement far outpaces that of developing countries.

The picture is further complicated with emerging economies increasingly determining the dynamics of energy markets, representing both opportunities for partnerships and challenges for growth that is compatible with environmental sustainability. According to the 2011 IEA World Energy Outlook, 90 percent of the projected growth in global energy demand over the next 25 years will come from non-OECD countries, with China alone accounting for more than 30 percent. Faster than Chinese rates of growth in energy consumption are Indian, Indonesian, Brazilian, and Middle Eastern demand. Global supply will also come to be dominated by emerging economies: the same report predicts that in 2035, non-OECD countries account for more than 70 percent of global gas production, particularly Russia, the Caspian, and Qatar.[166]

Given that developing countries are responsible for about half of the global CO_2 emissions today and are expected to be the primary polluters in the coming years,[167] reconciling the differences of the North–South divide and getting the developing countries on board is critical. It is with this need for equity in distribution of burden that the notion of "common but differentiated responsibility" has come to be, for better or for worse, central to international discussions on climate change, as seen in landmark documents such as the 1992 UN Framework Convention on Climate Change. But the issue is fraught with complications and nuances, and it remains to be seen how the North–South divide can be prevented from further defining how we meet the challenges of the new century.

Partnerships in emerging markets are surfacing within transitional contexts. As BRIC nations have rapidly developed, the notion of a North–South divide has been dramatically altered. Simultaneously, numerous nations in the global South remain largely as they were decades ago. Many of these economies have not grown substantially, and the health and economic challenges that have plagued these nations in recent years have persisted. Because these challenges have yet to be solved, new strategies are necessary. Moreover, even in the BRIC nations, rapid growth has created new challenges. Furthermore, these nations are now compelled to navigate how to maintain growth and serve populations with increased expectations.

STRATEGIC PARTNERSHIPS IN THE BRIC COUNTRIES

Bhavishya Alliance

The Bhavishya Alliance[168] is a partnership among organizations from the private, public and nonprofit sectors with the goal of halving the number of undernourished children in India by 2015.[169] Bhavishya facilitates cooperation between partners for pilot projects that address complex child under-nutrition problems.

In India, an estimated 75 million young children below 3 years old are undernourished.[170] The Bhavishya Alliance was created to redress this situation, and was originally created as the Partnership for Child Nutrition (PCN), initiated by the Synergos Institute, the United Nations Children's Fund (UNICEF) and Unilever. PCN was created to address the MDGs and reduce the number of undernourished children in India by 50 percent by 2015. The Alliance's most active partners are Unilever, HDFC Bank, ICICI Bank, the TATA Group, the State Health & Nutrition Mission, Integrated Child Development Scheme (ICDS), UNICEF, Health & Family Welfare Department, Women and Child Development Department, and leading NGOs.[171] Each partner contributes in different ways – providing core staff to develop programs, allocating infrastructure to the partnership's secretariat, financing the alliance's management, providing strategy guidance, and more.

The Bhavishya Alliance highly values monitoring and evaluation of its projects.[172] In some cases, the Alliance contracts out monitoring of its projects to independent third parties. In other cases, monitoring and evaluation is conducted in-house and its reports are published on the Alliance's website. Projects have been reviewed by the Shell Foundation and the Tata Institute of Social Science, among others.

Project Health Lokshakti – caring for mother and child[173]

Project Health Lokshakti is a multi-sector partnership of government officials, corporate representatives, civil society organizations and the community that supplements maternal and child health care services. The three-year pilot program is implemented in three stages and in two tribal blocks of Nashik district. The project includes setting up a helpline, providing transportation for maternal and infant emergencies, creating a flexi-pool at community level to meet emergency needs, and building capacities for medical and paramedical professionals and grassroots government personnel. The partners contribute in many ways. ICICI Lombard provides financial support and assistance on program branding; ICICI Foundation facilitates the program design, planning, and overall program management, as well as monitoring and evaluation; Vachan, the local NGO, is the implementer of the program in the field and monitors the day-to-day operations. The role of Bhavishya Alliance is to coordinate among partners and organize the overall management of the pilot program.

Thus far, the program has successfully implemented the following:

- The call center has been set up in the Vachan office at Nasik and operates 24/7 as a health Help Desk
- Transportation facilities have been established, and drivers received training
- The project was launched in Nasik.

Project Yashoda – behavioral change communications on infant feeding[174]

At the time of writing, Project Yashoda will soon be launched by the Bhavishya Alliance to target mothers and families of infants (aged six to twelve months) in Maharashtra's Nandurbar district. The goal of the initiative is to develop a comprehensive model to help children born in India receive wholesome and adequate nutrition through improved maternal awareness. The project attempts to instill complementary feeding behaviors among first-time mothers and families of infants. The project relies on Unilever's behavior change expertise and the technical knowledge of UNICEF and the State Nutrition Mission. The goal of the program is to educate mothers to start complementary feeding along with breastfeeding from the time the child is six months old and until the child is two years old. The project focuses on a communications mechanism that will be integrated into existing government structures and systems. The message will be comprehensible and will be conveyed through human-interest stories, films, radio messages, games, quizzes and more.

The content of the message was created by nutrition specialists from UNICEF and communications professionals from Hindustan Unilever Limited with the help of advertizing specialists from Ogilvy. The interventions will be executed by the ICDS, Health and Family Welfare Department. After the launch of the pilot, Bhavishya Alliance will conduct an evaluation of the impact of the communication tools, the delivery mechanism, and effectiveness of service providers' training.

Behavioral change on hand washing – two minutes for optimal hygiene[175]

The project was launched by Bhavishya in September 2008 to induce behavioral changes in hand washing that will increase sanitation practices and health in the area with the help of government programs and systems. The project capitalizes on the success of the Lifebuoy Swasthya Chetana (LBCS) model. The project was launched by Hindustan Unilever along with Ogilvy Action, who implemented the model on a larger scale.

The content of the LBCS model was integrated into existing public and nongovernmental preventative care programs. The pilot went on to becoming highly successful. The grassroots component of the program was executed by government agencies and NGOs. Unilever and Oglivy developed and adopted the behavior change communications model, while UNICEF served as a technical consultant on health and nutrition. Thus far, the hand washing program has been implemented in 214 villages, impacting 30,000 individuals. The pilot project was rolled out to three blocks in Nandurbar district and is expected to cover over 400 villages. In addition, 30 government trainers from Nandurbar and 45 volunteers were trained in the promotion of hand washing behavior.

Facility-based counseling program[176]

The Counselors Program is a partnership between the Department of Health and nonprofit organizations to improve the availability and access to health services at primary health centers.[177] Young Korku boys and girls serve as counselors who bridge between service providers and patients to ensure that the latter receive proper care and treatment and that the medical team understands their maladies. Twenty-four counselors, available 24 hours a day, seven days a week, have been instrumental in facilitating health and nutrition information to mothers arriving at primary health centers in Melghat. There are currently 24 Korku-speaking counselors working in 14 centers in Melghat.

Food diversification and hygiene education initiative – completed[178]

The Bhavishya Alliance identified that the government-run Supplementary Nutrition Programme (SNP) suffered from inadequate variety, nutritional quality, hygiene and awareness in many places in India. In order to supplement the SNP, the Alliance facilitated a food diversification and hygiene education initiative in Nandurbar by utilizing experts from corporate and civil society. In particular, the Bhavishya Alliance relied on the expertise of the Taj Hotels, Institute of Hotel Management, and the Rajmata Jijau Mother-Child Health and Nutrition Mission to steer the program.

After studying local cooking habits and ingredients and visiting local tribes, chefs from the Taj Group of Hotels developed over 37 recipes within the strict requirements of the government's program. Each portion had to cost less than Rs. 2 per child per day and provide 300 Kcal and 8 grams of protein. The Institute of Hotel Management, Aurangabad, developed a system for training trainers, parent groups and self-help groups on recipe preparation and skills to conduct grassroots advocacy. After the success of the pilot project, the initiative was replicated across many districts in Maharashtra and other states.

The initiatives' successes include:

- Almost 12,000 government community workers trained in preparing diverse recipes and managing nutritional programs
- Food diversity steadily increased in 88 percent of locations in the district
- Roughly 93 percent of food centers began serving hot food following the intervention
- Ninety-seven percent of centers now clean their utensils before cooking, compared with 31 percent of centers before intervention.

Day Care Centers at construction sites initiative – completed[179]

The Bhavishya Alliance particularly wished to help the children of migrant construction workers by launching the Day Care Centers initiative. The Alliance urged the ICDS to extend nutritional care to children of migrant workers. As a result, the ICDS Commissioner authorized setting up temporary nutrition centers in construction sites across Mumbai.

The Bhavishya Alliance piloted three day care nutrition centers that were supported by the government (through ICDS), B.G. Shirke Group of Companies, and two NGOs – Mumbai Mobile Creches and Nirman. The partners developed center programs with extended hours, trained staff, supervised the management of centers, and contributed funds and infrastructure – real estate, electricity, drinking water, and sanitation. In addition, 530 children were administered BCG, DPT, measles, MMR and TT vaccines during health camps conducted by primary health centers. The three centers helped 1459 children in one year, 1006 of which were under six years old. The program decreased the percentage of severely malnourished children from 11.5 percent to 3.5 percent in two of the three centers. In order to ensure the long-term provision of nutritional supplements to children, the Alliance facilitated the formation of self-help parental networks.

Computer Aided Adult Literacy Health and Nutrition Awareness Program – completed[180]

To battle poor nutrition and health practices due to lack of awareness and illiteracy of mothers, the Alliance initiated a pilot program that worked to improve female literacy in India. The Alliance partnered with the Integrated Tribal Welfare Department (ITDP) of the national government, the Vachan NGO, and TCS, a private company, to implement 30 community centers in the Nasik District. The partnership was successful such that 350 women became functionally literate and aware of good health and nutrition practices. A total of 1063 women and adolescents were covered under the literacy program, and 63 percent of the target group became functionally literate. Other improved measurements include pregnancy registration at PHC, which increased from 1 to 45 percent, an increase in breastfeeding from 2 to 54 percent, and an overall increase in awareness of the importance in the retention of immunization cards from 28 to 86 percent. In its conclusions, the partnership stated that severe power cuts impeded the work of the centers, and that success was often dependent on familial support.

This partnership demonstrates the potential of strategic collaboration to leverage resources to meet a social need. Additionally, it is positioned to inform government, and increase its effectiveness. It seeds the approaches that government can eventually institutionalize. It is not easy for government to initiate pilot projects with lasting consequences without some outside support and involvement. In this respect, Bhavishya fills an important void. This circumstance underscores the potential value of nongovernmental efforts to test ideas and strategies that government can institutionalize. External nimble efforts can flexibly experiment through trial and error, and hone approaches that can shape public policy.

Global Alliance for TB Drug Development

The Global Alliance for TB Drug Development (TB Alliance or GATB) is a nonprofit, product development partnership (PDP) organization that brings together public, private, academic, and philanthropic sectors to develop new, simpler, fast-acting TB drug regimens. Established in 2000 in Cape Town, South Africa, the formation of the TB Alliance responded to the need for faster, better, and affordable TB treatments; at the time, there were none in clinical development, dashing hopes for improved medication for patients of one of the world's deadliest pandemic diseases. According to the World Health Organization, tuberculosis is the greatest killer worldwide due to a single infection agent after HIV/AIDS, with 8.8 million people falling ill with the disease in 2010 and 1.4 million dying from it the same year. Over 95 percent of such deaths take place in low- and middle-income countries,[181] making the establishment of the TB Alliance in South Africa particularly pertinent.

Called "a shining example of public and private sector partnerships to bridge the gap between market opportunities and people's needs"[182] by then Director General of the World Health Organization, Dr. Gro Harlem Brundtland, the TB Alliance is a virtual drug developer. It manages a portfolio of candidate TB compounds from public and private sector sources and uses a range of licensing and partnership agreements. External research facilities and contractors carry out the bulk of the laboratory and clinical work, though the TB Alliance directly maintains the management oversight of projects. This model is designed to mini- mize costs (including for overhead and infrastructure investments) and accelerate drug development.[183]

According to its website, the TB Alliance offers the greatest concen- tration of TB drug development expertise in the world, including more than 20 active development programs, with three compounds in late-stage clinical testing. As a central resource for global TB drug development, the TB Alliance has lowered the barriers associated with the field, thereby promoting its reinvigoration. As a result, there are now ten clinical TB drug candidates being developed globally, many of which are managed by the world's leading pharmaceutical companies.

In addition, it cofounded the Critical Path to TB Drug Regimens (CPTR) initiative, which aims to speed the development of new and improved drug regimens for the disease by bringing together the world's leading drug developers, global regulatory agencies, and civil society organizations. As the leader of the drug development arm of the program, the TB Alliance has helped reduce the timeline for TB regimen development by as much as 75 percent. Among its prominent partnerships are: first-ever parallel development program of a TB drug candidate for drug-sensitive and drug-resistant indications in collaboration with Janssen Pharmaceuticals (of Johnson & Johnson), and the first-ever royalty-free license agreement between two nonprofits, in partnership with Drugs for Neglected Diseases initiative (DNDi), to test and develop compounds to treat multiple additional neglected diseases.[184]

Guangdong Environmental Partnership Program

The Guangdong Environmental Partnership Program was launched in 2007 by the Institute for Sustainable Communities (ISC),[185] an organization focused on helping communities around the world tackle environmental, economic and social challenges.[186] The Guangdong Environmental Partnership Program (the Partnership) is a public private partnership that was created to reduce greenhouse gas emissions, improve public health, and increase environmental accountability in the Guangdong Province of China, which is commonly referred to as the "factory of the world".

The Partnership engages with NGOs, businesses and governments in activities that build skills, awareness and motivation to work collaboratively on environmental issues. The Partnership hopes to instigate change in environmental and energy-efficient practices across all sectors in Guangdong.

The Partnership receives financial support from the United States Agency of International Development (USAID) through a Congressional earmark.[187] "This partnership harnesses both Chinese and American innovation with a common goal: to establish Guangdong as a regional leader in clean energy and sustainable growth," said Olivier Carduner, the Director of USAID's Regional Development Mission to China.[188] In addition to USAID, the Partnership engages with high-power private sector companies and foundations that contribute finances and expertise to the success of the programs. These include General Electric, GE Foundation, Citi Foundation, Wal-Mart, Rockefeller Brothers Fund, Honeywell, SABIC Innovative Plastics, Adidas, and Japan Foundation Center for Global Partnership.[189] ISC works with Chinese local authorities and partners to implement the Partnership's programs. The Partnership also works with the following organizations: Business for Social Responsibility, the Global Environmental Institute, the Guangdong Economic and Trade Commission, Guangdong Environmental Protection Bureau, LEAF (Japan), Lingnan College, Sun Yat-sen University, Ministry of Environmental Protection, National Development and Reform Commission, Natural Resources Defense Council, Shelburne Farms, Shining Stone, South China Normal University, Doumen Township, Guanlan Township, Sanjiao Township, US EPA, and Vermont Law School.

The Partnership implements three major initiatives: Environment, Health and Safety (EHS) education, environmental governance, and community mobilization. The EHS initiatives take place in EHS Academies, set up by the Partnership to educate factory managers on measures that can save energy, reduce harmful emissions, and improve worker health safety conditions.[190] The academies help improve the ability of factories, suppliers, and small- and medium-size businesses to reduce their harmful emissions and comply with environmental regulation.

ISC established the first EHS Academy in Guangdong in 2007, and following its success launched a second academy in 2010.[191] The first academy is located in the Sun Yat-sen University's Lingman College – a business school – in order to build domestic capacity to manage the robust EHS practices in China. The training curriculum was based on best practices from GE, Honeywell and Adidas. Experts from the corporations, along with Chinese experts, also developed the curriculum under the guidance of an international steering committee.[192] In its first 18 months, the EHS Academy trained over 3500 managers.[193] With two academies in operations, the Partnership anticipates they will train at least 4000 managers per year.

The academies are hoping to achieve the following results:

- Companies in China will increase their compliance with Chinese and international standards
- Workflow interruptions due to injury will decrease
- Businesses will consume less energy
- Local environments will be better protected
- Greenhouse gases (GHG) and other harmful emissions will be reduced in the province.[194]

In 2009 the Guangdong Bureau of Labor and Social Security officially endorsed the EHS Academy and began working with its administrators and experts to develop Chinese professional, government-sanctioned EHS certification protocols. The Ministry of Environmental Protection is also involved in the work of the academies.[195] More than 24 international corporations are already taking advantage of the EHS Academy system, including Starbucks, GE, Nike, Honda, Dell, Timberland, and Wal-Mart.

The second initiative of the Partnership focuses on environmental governance. The Partnership works to strengthen the capacity of the South China Environmental Protection Supervision Center and regional environmental protection institutions to implement regulation, provide public information, and engage with community members.[196] For this initiative, the Partnership enlisted the help of the US Environmental Protection Agency. In 2010, leaders from Guangdong power companies and the Power Generation Group, which oversees power generation plants in the province, visited local power plants in the US to learn about best practices for energy efficiency and emissions control.[197] The delegation met with experts from the US utility companies, energy and emissions control experts from Johnson Controls, World Resources Institute, Lawrence Berkeley National Laboratory, the US Department of Energy, and the US Environmental Protection Agency.

The Partnership's third initiative works to mobilize communities on environmental protection and energy efficiency. The Partnership launched projects in three communities that demonstrate the relationship between energy efficiency and health and cost-of-living concerns.[198] The projects provide information to the public on environmental accountability and transparency. The Partnership hopes to inspire community-wide initiatives that will exceed energy efficiency targets by engaging with city employees, businesses, schools, NGOs and community leaders. ISC is also developing courses on resource efficiency and environmental health for children aged nine to thirteen years.[199]

This partnership harnesses expertise from various resources across sectors. Learning from best practices informs new thinking about the environment in a region in need of substantial progress in this area.

Urban Water Partnerships – UN-HABITAT and Coca-Cola

In March 2010, UN-HABITAT and Coca-Cola signed an agreement[200] to improve community access to clean drinking water and adequate sanitation services in countries in Asia, Africa and South America.[201] "Clean water and sanitation is the key to human development and are the basic requirements to improving the living conditions of the urban poor." This new partnership is a continuation of a previous partnership signed between UN-HABITAT and Coca-Cola India & South West Asia in April 2007 to improve access to safe drinking water and sanitation in India and Nepal under the Water for Asian Cities Programme.[202] The 2010 partnership planned to establish operations in Bangladesh, Pakistan and India.

Both partners will together identify and pursue projects to improve access to safe drinking water. Both organizations committed equal contributions to the $1 million partnership.

The 2007 partnership required each organization to commit $150,000 over three years to implement pilot demonstration projects in India and Nepal. The partnership focused on the following activities:

1. Improving water management, hygiene and sanitation in specific poor urban areas in Nepal
2. Increasing operations of water storage and conservation in schools in selected cities in Madhya Pradesh, India
3. Providing safe drinking water and sanitation to urban poor populations in West Bengal, India, focusing on schools by promoting and installing household- and community-managed water treatment centers
4. Implementing programs to increase awareness on water usage, sanitation, and conservation including mobilization of political will and capacity building among students and political leaders.

The partnership launched a water conservation program in Madhya Pradesh, access to potable water program in West Bengal, and awareness of water and sanitation program in Nepal. The partnership executed the programs in schools that took over operations once the programs were fully implemented.

Madhya Pradesh
In Madhya Pradesh the local government made rooftop rainwater harvesting mandatory for all buildings in municipal areas with a plot size of over 250 meters^2.[203] To assist residents, the government offered a rebate on the annual property tax for the year in which the rainwater harvesting facilities are installed. In Madhya Pradesh, the Lake Conservation Authority (LCA) is representing the region in the partnership. LCA also contributed cash and in-kind donations to help leverage more sources for the partnership.

The pilot project was launched in 16 schools in four cities. At the conclusion of the project in January 2010, responsibility for the operations of the rainwater harvesting facilities and the educational programs on water safety, conservation, hygiene and sanitation were turned over to the schools. Due to the success of the program, the School Education Department of the Government of Madhya Pradesh expressed the need to replicate the program in other schools by using the state's resources.

Nepal

In Nepal, the partnership focused on implementing household water treatment (HWT) technologies, such as chlorination and solar water disinfection, in urban areas in the country. The partnership also supplemented the efforts of UNICEF and the Department of Water Supply and Sewerage to increase awareness of the relationship between safe water and reducing water-borne illness. The program increased awareness and educated the population as well as reinforced the capacity of local producers of HWT technology. The project was launched by UN-HABITAT, Bottlers Nepal Limited and local authorities in 2008.

Several organizations contributed funds to the partnership. In addition to UN-HABITAT and Coca-Cola India, the Environment and Public Health Organisation, Bottlers Nepal Limited and local authorities and governments also made financial contributions to the partnership's programs.[204] At the conclusion of activity, 13 communities were declared as Safe Water Zones and incidences of water-borne illnesses were reduced in the communities that implemented the program.

West Bengal

The objective of the initiative in West Bengal was to provide access to safe drinking water and sanitation for the urban poor, placing an emphasis on providing potable water to 100 schools that are located in water-scarce zones.[205] The partners were UN-HABITAT, Coca-Cola and the Communication and Capacity Development Unit under the Public Health Engineering Department, the latter of which executed the project. In 2009, the partnership conducted an assessment in 150 schools in West Bengal, selecting 100 applicants. The provision of sustainable water systems in schools was completed in 2010. The government partner also reached out to Charabedia Rural Economic and Area Development Society to implement the project in their regional area of operations. Once systems were installed, they were turned over to the schools for operations and maintenance.

This partnership has achieved demonstrable results due to a contractual arrangement between UN-HABITAT and Coca-Cola.

Grow Africa Partnership

Launched under the joint auspices of the African Union, New Partnership for Africa's Development (NEPAD), and the WEF, Grow Africa is a partnership platform designed to accelerate sustainable investments in African agriculture for improved food security. Agriculture is recognized as the central component of economic growth and poverty alleviation in

Africa that promotes food security and reduction of hunger.[206] As such, improved agriculture represents a key tool to achieving the first UN MDG to eradicate extreme poverty and hunger.

Grow Africa was initiated at the WEF on Africa in May 2011. It is built on the public private partnership pilot models of the WEF's New Vision for Agriculture Initiative.

Grow Africa's role is threefold:

- **Increase private sector investments**: by helping partner countries in the development of their investment blueprints, pipelines of investments, and cross sector collaboration, Grow Africa works to channel private sector investment into African agriculture.
- **Enable multi-stakeholder partnerships**: by facilitating exchange of best practices and stakeholder engagement in order to merge local and international stakeholder capacities, Grow Africa helps attract investments in initiatives that complement national agricultural strategies and support the implementation of the Comprehensive African Agricultural Development Programme (CAADP). The CAADP is a program of NEPAD to boost agricultural productivity in Africa by bringing together key players at the continental, regional, and national levels to coordinate and share experiences. Its mission is to improve food security, nutrition, and increase incomes in Africa's largely farming-based economies. To this end, it sets a goal of raising agricultural productivity by a minimum of 6 percent and increasing public investment in agriculture to 10 percent of national budgets a year.[207]
- **Expand knowledge and awareness of best practices and existing initiatives**: Grow Africa works to increase investor interest in agriculture by sharing information and lessons from existing and successful projects, as well as by addressing important issues such as gender inclusion, land tenure, climate change, and resource management.

The following are some examples of country initiatives across Africa for multi-stakeholder partnerships that promote investment in agriculture in alignment with national priorities.

Agricultural Growth Project (AGP) in Ethiopia
AGP is a comprehensive strategy for the transformation of Ethiopia's agricultural sector into a market-led sector in order to achieve food security, environmental conservation, as well as gender inclusion and equity. It is hoped that the country will reach middle-income status by

2020. To carry out AGP's work, an independent body was established, the Agricultural Transformation Agency (ATA). Its role is to create an enabling environment, improve industry structure and engage the private sector, increase productivity of smallholder farmers, improve frontline extension quality, and scale irrigation and improved land management.[208]

Southern Agricultural Growth Corridor of Tanzania (SAGCOT)
In a country where agriculture is the basis of its economy, SAGCOT promotes "clusters" of profitable agricultural farming and services businesses that benefit small-scale farmers and thereby improve food security, reduce rural poverty, and promote environmental sustainability. By bringing together the government, businesses, donor partners, and the farming community, SAGCOT allows for the pooling of resources and collaboration.[209] Tanzania's vast natural resources and its strategic location make it attractive for commercial investment, and SAGCOT hopes to leverage this.[210]

Lamu Port – South Sudan – Ethiopia Transport Corridor (LAPSSET), Kenya
In Kenya, agriculture provides 80 percent of rural employment, 26 percent of its GDP, and 45 percent of government revenues. The LAPSSET takes part of the country's Agricultural Sector Development Strategy (ASDS), which commits public investment in Kenyan agriculture. The LAPSSET is undertaking vast infrastructural improvements along a corridor linking Lamu Port to regional markets in South Sudan, Ethiopia, and others. The new infrastructures will be developed to support six growth areas that have high potential for agriculture.[211]

9.   The rural challenge

Expanded urbanization has altered rural environments. Growing cities sprawl into rural areas. Rural residents move to cities seeking employment. Demand shifts to cities, and rural environments must adapt accordingly. Societies that were once primarily agrarian have substantially modernized, altering the context of rural communities. Many small farmers could improve production and marketing in this context, but they often lack access to the technology and resources to strengthen their capacity.

The Millennium Summit and its resulting MDGs thrust poverty reduction as a principal development goal of our century. Mass poverty is not only a problem for the poor themselves – it translates into economic loss (underutilized talent and resources), threatens social stability and civil order, and acts a festering ground for communicable diseases in impoverished areas, to name a few. As the International Fund for Agricultural Development (IFAD) indicated, "Nobody, rich or poor, can remain immune from the consequences."[212]

If the world is to halve the proportion of people suffering from extreme poverty and hunger between 1990 and 2015, as MDG 1 suggests, then we must understand poverty's many facets. One of the most glaring aspects of poverty, though perhaps not always appreciated by the general public, is that it remains heavily rural. According to the World Bank, 75 percent of the developing world's poor live in rural areas, when only 58 percent of its population is rural.[213] In these rural areas, agriculture is the primary mode of making a living, and agricultural growth has been cited to generate the greatest improvements for the poorest.

One percent growth in GDP stemming from agriculture increases the expenditures of the poorest 30 percent of the population at least two and a half times as much as growth elsewhere in the economy.[214] Between 1993 and 2002, the World Bank estimates that rural poverty reduction contributed more than 45 percent to overall poverty reduction, with rural–urban migration accounting for only a small percentage of this.[215] Yet, agriculture has arguably not always received the emphasis commensurate with its impact – IFAD reports that though the figure has since increased slightly, agriculture received only around 3 percent of the total Official Development Assistance between 2003 and 2006.[216]

Furthermore, rural areas also play a key role in another important challenge: climate change mitigation. As day-to-day managers of many of the ecosystems (for example as farmers, fishers, forest dwellers), the rural poor are in a unique position to conserve. As a result, it is critical to ensure rural dwellers access to the rights and resources necessary for sustaining livelihoods to maintain the health of ecosystems in the face of climate change.[217] Consequently, rural poverty reduction is a global priority with potentially far-reaching benefits. Innovation in agricultural production and direct intervention to further develop impoverished rural communities are crucial strategies to strengthen rural contexts. This reality suggests cooperation across sectors to ensure coordinated effort across local governments, international agencies, corporations, rural dwellers, and a range of other partners.

ANGOLA PARTNERSHIP INITIATIVE

The Angola Partnership Initiative (API) was launched in 2006 by ChevronTexaco Corp. (Chevron), USAID, the United National Development Programme (UNDP) and the Government of Angola.[218] API was established with a $50 million budget to support education, training, and small-business development in Angola. The partners' common goal is to promote sustainable economic and social development in Angola.

API projects pursue long-term sustainable development, rather than meeting short-term philanthropic needs.[219] Projects are participatory, leveraging existing funds and expertise within different organizations. The effort features two main programs – the Municipal Development Program and the Agricultural Development and Finance Program.

Municipal Development Program

The Municipal Development Program supports the Government of Angola's efforts to bolster its local institutional capacity. The program aligns with Angola's recent shift towards decentralization of government and engaging more with the public. The Municipal Development Program, launched and supported by USAID, Chevron and the Angolan Ministry of Territorial Administration, benefits selected municipalities in Bié, Cabina, Cuando Cubango, and Huambo.[220] Lazare Kaplan International partners with USAID to implement the program in Lunda Norte.

The program includes three parts:

1. Technical assistance and training to community members that improves their engagement in the preparation and implementation of local development plans
2. Technical assistance and on-the-job training to municipal employees on planning processes, effectively managing planning sessions and budgets, and monitoring the delivery of public services
3. A municipal development fund to support construction and rehabilitation of community infrastructure.

Chevron and USAID established the Enterprise Development Alliance to provide technical assistance and financial support to small enterprises in Angola, emphasizing the agriculture and water sectors. Each organization provides matching funds, with an original funding commitment of $20 million. The agreement alliance is executed by a private-management investment fund called the Angola Enterprise Fund. The Fund's programs focus on vocational training and job creation for small- and medium-size enterprises in Angola. The Fund attracts private funds, with matching funding commitments, for an overall fundraising target of $10 million.

Agricultural Development and Finance Program

The goal of the Agricultural Development and Finance Program is to catalyze the value chain of selected agricultural products, from production to processing to marketing, including support for the financial sector along the value chain. Growth in the agriculture sector is an important element in generating broad-based economic growth in Angola in the near term. The Agriculture Development and Finance Program, also known as ProAgro Angola, was launched in 2007.[221] ProAgro Angola is a partnership between Chevron, USAID and the Ministry of Agriculture and Rural Development. ProAgro Angola establishes connections in the market and increases access to financial services for farmers and agribusinesses. The program improves the dialogue between agriculture enterprises, the Angolan government and private sector counterparts. The program also helps strengthen production, processing, buying and selling of agricultural products.

ProAgro has four components:

1. Expanding access to financial services for farmers and agribusinesses: ProAgro facilitates sustainable relationships between commercial banks and agriculture enterprises. The program is

supported by a USAID guarantee facility, covering 25 percent of a $15 million loan portfolio for agribusiness at Banco de Fomento Angola.

2.   Enhancing the productivity and production of selected crops: ProAgro provides technical assistance to increase yields and improve crop quality. The program emphasizes integrated pest management, modern crop husbandry techniques, crop scheduling, soil protection, irrigation, and water management.

3.   Improving processes and practices: the program provides technical assistance to make improvements in areas such as sorting and grading, packaging, safe transportation of fruits and vegetables, and storage.

4.   Improving marketing strategies: ProAgro assists farmers and agri-businesses to identify market opportunities, improve marketing strategies, use market information systems, and form business contracts and alliances.

ProAgro helps banana growers in the Benguela and Bengo provinces organize into cooperatives.[222] In the first two years, the farmers nearly doubled their yields.

Since 1989, Chevron has been involved in a host of programs and initiatives in Angola. Chevron has invested more than $160 million in programs in Angola that support public health, education, and economic, environmental and social needs.[223] Many of the programs are managed in cooperation with USAID, the Angolan government, and other related organizations.

Health
Chevron focuses its efforts on the health of women and children. Chevron and its partners support the Cabinda Blood Bank, which helps fight blood-transmitted diseases. In 2010, the Bank facilitated more than 11,800 safe blood transfusions in the Cabinda province. The partners also provide drugs, supplies and x-ray equipment for the Cabinda Tuberculosis Program, which operates in 20 health centers throughout the province. Thus far, the Cabinda Tuberculosis Program has treated more than 600 patients. In the Cabinda province, Chevron also works to prevent mother-to-child HIV transmission. In 2010, more than 200 babies received milk supplements twice per month. Finally, in an effort to eradicate polio in Angola, Chevron contributed nearly $950,000 to help vaccinate one million children and adults.

Education
Chevron engages in educational programs in the regions where it
operates. In partnership with the Discovery Channel and the Ministry of
Education, Chevron helps improve the quality of teaching in Angola's
elementary and secondary schools with the use of video technology. The
Discovery Channel Global Education Partnership has reached over
66,000 students since it was launched in 2004. Chevron also finances a
variety of innovative education programs and contributes to scholarship
funds for Cabinda-based university students.

Building human capacity
Chevron supports social investment programs that improve the overall
capacity of individuals and organizations in Angola. In 2010, Chevron
sponsored two "Shaping the Way We Teach English" workshops in
Cabinda that introduced 85 English teachers to new educational tools.

Agriculture and fishing
In addition to its involvement in ProAgro, Chevron promotes several
agriculture programs that improve the livelihood and operations of
farmers in Angola. Chevron is involved in the Integrated Agriculture
Project, promoting crops that improve food security and reduce poverty
among rural populations. The Integrated Agriculture Project promotes
bananas, cassava, Irish potatoes and sweet potatoes. With the assistance
of Chevron, an agriculture initiative in Cabina taught 554 farmers better
agriculture techniques, helping small farmers use modern agriculture
techniques and increase their access to markets. The project concluded in
May 2010 with the creation of a farmer-owned cooperative. Chevron also
supports programs that improve fishermen's earning power and safety.
More than 2700 fishermen have already taken part in the programs.

Small enterprise development
Chevron and its partners have operated the Banco BAI Microfinanças,
formally known as NovoBanco, since 2004. Banco BAI Microfinanças is
a microfinance institution that supports small entrepreneurs in Angola.
By the end of 2010, the bank had made almost $54 million in loans. In
2010 alone, the bank provided loans in the sum of $9.9 million to 418
female entrepreneurs.

   In this partnership, one corporation has immersed itself in comprehensive development, collaborating with local partners in a country of
strategic importance to its business. Indeed, with its own self-interest in
mind, Chevron has collaborated to strengthen opportunities for rural
communities. The health and wellbeing of Angola can only assist

Chevron's business goals. The symbiotic arrangement is very much characteristic of contemporary strategic cross sector partnerships.

AHP-CII-UK – ABORIGINAL LEADERSHIP INITIATIVE

Ahp-cii-uk – the Aboriginal Leadership Initiative – is a cross sector partnership created to improve the ability of Aboriginal communities in Canada, government agencies, businesses and nonprofit organizations to "collaborate on projects that improve the quality of life for indigenous peoples."[224] The Aboriginal Leadership Initiative focuses on building long-term relationships between First Nations – Aboriginal communities in rural Canada – and non-Aboriginal partners ("First Nations" refers collectively to various indigenous people within Canada with different cultures, languages, histories and social structures). The partnership develops social and economic projects at the grassroots level.[225] Ahp-cii-uk works with three Aboriginal communities – Ahousaht, Tseshaht, and Ehattesaht – to bridge the gaps between the resources they have and their ability to access them. Ahp-cii-uk was created to address problems that have long been addressed by national policies but failed to make a significant impact on poverty, employment, housing, water and infrastructure conditions, isolation from other communities, family intergenerational conflicts, and poor diets.

In 2004 a series of conversations took place between senior government officials, business leaders, and Aboriginal communities and organizations. The result of these conversations was the creation of the partnership that later gave rise to the Aboriginal Leadership Initiative, with a pilot program in British Columbia called Ahp-cii-uk. The partnership is meant to strengthen the capacity of First Nations to ultimately become self-sustaining on issues of economic development and social programming. The initiative's goals are to create a positive social and economic change in First Nations; to teach partners new ways of working with First Nations communities; to strengthen the self-sufficiency and health of the communities; and to spread this model of partnership across British Columbia and Canada. The initiative is effective because it builds long-term relationships between multiple partners, works with interested individuals, and takes a holistic approach.

Ahp-cii-uk is based on four pillars:[226]

1.   Capacity building: increasing the ability of Aboriginal communities to initiate, manage, and participate in community development programs.

2. Dialogue and trust-building: deepening the understanding between Aboriginal and non-Aboriginal partners, bridging divides and building new relationships.
3. Action initiatives: enabling cross sector teams to design and implement concrete pilot projects that directly respond to the communities' needs.
4. Evaluation and replication: assessing results, documenting learning and replicating successful initiatives in other geographical areas.

The initiative selects projects according to three guiding principles:[227]

- Projects that focus on the strengths and opportunities the community believes will have a positive impact
- Projects that will help build the capacity of community members to make effective decisions and manage projects
- Projects that rely on consensus decision-making and that lead to a continuous accommodation of the community's interests.

The partnership was launched by four initiating partners:

1. Nuu-chah-nulth Tribal Council (provides services and programs to approximately 8,000 registered members, including child welfare, fisheries, economic development, education and training, financial administrative support, employment and training, infrastructure development, health, communications, and social development)
2. Health Canada
3. British Columbia Ministry of Aboriginal Relations and Reconciliation
4. Synergos Institute (an independent nonprofit organization that supports leaders and partnerships to change systems that keep people in poverty).

Health Canada and the British Columbia Ministry of Aboriginal Relations and Reconciliation provide funding for the initiative. Other partners include:

- From the government: BC Ministry of Aboriginal Relations and Reconciliation, Indian and Northern Affairs Canada
- From the business and nonprofit sectors: BC Hydro, Ecotrust Canada, Fortis BC, Nuu-chah-nulth Economic Development Corporation, Port Metro Vancouver, RBC, TD Canada Trust, Vancity

- Financial contributors: Coulson Forest Products, Donner Canadian Foundation, Ethos JWT, First People's World Wide, BC Hydro.

Monitoring and evaluation of the partnership's performance and approach to community development is conducted by independent evaluators. The Donner Canadian Foundation contributed funding and in early 2008 the New Development Economy Group was hired to conduct the evaluation. Representatives from the New Development Economy Group visited the communities several times, observed meetings and conducted interviews with community members, external partners and the initiative's staff. The evaluation was conducted through a qualitative study. Its main findings are as follows:

1. The initiative is unique and new in the sense that it focuses on building trust and respect between partners. It is linked to culture and seeks to reinforce self-esteem.
2. The strength of the relationships is at the core of the partnership's success. Partners exhibit signs of a strong commitment to the collaboration.
3. Initial community skepticism is being overcome.
4. Local engagement is slowly growing.
5. The community's awareness of the partnership is building.
6. There are apparent changes in behavior and attitudes.
7. There is an increased willingness to listen to other points of view.
8. The initiative is helping the community come together.
9. Fundamental progress has been made to build relationships and trust.

Specific projects in the communities of Ahp-cii-uk include:

In Tseshaht[228]

The Tseshaht community decided to launch two major projects – an artists' market and a spiritual healing center. Artists in the community recognized the potential for increasing their exposure opportunities with the support of Ahp-cii-uk. First, local artists presented their work in a local bar. Next, the community began building a local art gallery. In addition, the Nuu-chah-nulth Economic Development Corporation began offering micro-loans, workshops and other support services to First Nations artists to help them develop their portfolios and inventory.

The spiritual center was created in response to a desire within the community to support the healing process of individuals with addictions.

In addition to the spiritual center, community members also formed a prayer group and a parents' support group for the population struggling from addiction problems. Finally, the community organized a series of activities for the 2008 holiday season that provided "wholesome family fun free of drugs and alcohol."[229]

Following a deadly car accident in 2009 in which a young boy was hit by a vehicle while riding his bicycle, the community engaged in a host of activities to increase road safety. Community members cleared roads and placed signs that remind drivers they are driving through residential neighborhoods. The community also worked with the Ministry of Transport to make changes to the roads and purchased road-side speed monitoring equipment. The community Road Safety Task Force was successful in reducing the speed limit and implementing better road signage in Tseshaht.

In Ehattesaht[230]

The Ehattesaht community recognized the need for life skills training that will help locals live up to their full potential. The Nuu-chah-nulth Employment and Training Program runs the life skills and pre-employment program in the community. The course is eight weeks long, and for the first session the initiative's local coordinator was successful in enlisting 12 community members to enroll. The course's graduates showed considerable growth in the skills they need to succeed, and strengthened their belief that achieving their goals, which include opening a community store or a day care center, is possible.

Graduates of the program were given the opportunity to launch new programs to promote community development. The graduates worked with council members to plan the beautification of community spaces. The group conducted a garbage cleanup and built a children's playground.

The Ehattesaht community has seen an increase in the number of people involved in the initiative's meetings and conversations. With the help of Ahp-cii-uk, two young men from the reserve took part in a traditional reconciliation ceremony, which proved to be a healing event between families. The facilitator that conducted the ceremony instructed the community on the proceedings should they decide to conduct the ceremony again in the future.

In Ahousaht[231]

The Ahousaht community chose to focus on revitalizing the Walk the Wild Heritage Trail. Community members expressed a desire to revitalize the trail in order to attract tourism to the area. Several organizations became involved, and the project secured funds from local businesses and other funding sources. Ahp-cii-uk partnered with BC Parks, and with the help of BC Conservation Corps, hired four individuals to work on the trail. The four employees were hired locally with the help of Ahp-cii-uk coordinators, who provided assistance to community members in their application process.

Revitalizing the trail also provided opportunities for promoting local artistry. Community artists participated in a contest to develop a trail logo. The community also secured funding for a local master carver to carve a Welcome Figure for the head of the trail. Now the community focuses on marketing the trail to increase tourism activity.

The initiative also helped developing personal capacity in Ahousaht. When the local partnership coordinator was feeling overwhelmed by her responsibilities, the community helped find her a mentor. Over time, the coordinator gained confidence in public speaking, creating meeting agendas and developed good organizational skills.

Collaboration across difference is hardly automatic. As demonstrated in this partnership's experiences, building trust has been a prerequisite for any actual program development. Especially in environments with historic inequality and oppression between groups, collaboration may be far from anyone's conscience. It takes time to build relationships. As indicated in the evaluation of the partnership, much of the effort's progress emphasizes overcoming skepticism, and building trust and relationships.

Overall, partnerships in rural contexts operate in unique circumstances, as they must adapt to deep traditions. They work with populations that have not experienced as much rapid change as communities in urban environments, yet they are, in some ways, left behind by urbanization. They need substantial technological and infrastructure upgrades to compete. Ways of life that are long held may be in jeopardy in numerous rural environments. Partnerships must respect existing cultures, yet address real contemporary needs.

PART III

Partnerships around critical issues of global significance

10. Meeting the climate change challenge

Exceptional global population growth and altered economic circumstances have exerted additional pressure on the environment, with the planet now counting over seven billion inhabitants and the global economic output increasing twenty fold.[232] Rapidly rising demand and consumption of energy have driven global warming and climate change. Between 1990 and 2007, world gross domestic product increased 156 percent, accompanied by a 39 percent increase in global energy demand, resulting in a 38 percent rise in global CO_2 emissions.[233] In 2010, globally averaged mixing ratios of greenhouse gases reached new highs, according the World Meteorological Organization.[234]

Currently,[235] according to the International Energy Agency, the top CO_2 emitting countries are:

1. China
2. the US
3. India
4. Russia
5. Japan
6. Germany
7. Iran
8. Canada
9. South Korea
10. the UK.

These top ten emitters account for approximately two-thirds of the world's CO_2 emissions.[236] The largest five emitters (China, US, India, Russia, and Japan) comprised 45 percent of the total global population and produced 56 percent of the global CO_2 emissions in 2009.[237] Emerging economies are responsible for the net growth in global energy consumption growth, with China alone accounting for 71 percent, according to the BP Statistical Review of World Energy (June 2012). Meanwhile, energy consumption by OECD countries, led by Japan, declined.[238] The highest levels of emissions per GDP are observed in the Middle East and the Economies in Transition (EIT).

It is also important to note the nuances in the figures: for example, the large share of the US emissions in the overall global total is commensurate with its share of economic output, as measured by GDP. Meanwhile Japan's emissions is proportionately 29 percent less than that of Russia, when considering that its GDP is more than double that of Russia.

While reaching emission reduction targets globally has been elusive, some improvements have been made: for example, if we consider CO_2 emissions *per unit of GDP*, among the top five, China, Russia, and the US have significantly reduced their CO_2 emissions per GDP between 1990 and 2009 (China's emissions per GDP have fallen close to the level of the US), while India and Japan already had much lower emissions per GDP, according to the IEA.[239]

DURBAN INDUSTRY CLIMATE CHANGE PARTNERSHIP PROJECT

In 2009 the United Nations Industrial Development Organization (UNIDO) partnered with several Durban organizations to create a climate change strategy for this metropolitan center. The key goal of the project was to create a mechanism for the private sector in Durban that responds to climate change risks and opportunities.[240] The project, structured in three phases, took place between June 2009 and June 2010. It brought together the public and private sector to address the current climate debate and create possible solutions for mitigating climate change in South Africa.

The project was implemented by UNIDO and its partners – the Durban Investment Promotion Agency (DIPA), the eThekwini Municipality, and the Durban Chamber of Commerce. Identified industries are seen as essential for enhanced climate change activities. These include the automotive, petroleum and chemicals, and the maritime and logistics industries.

The first stage of the project focused on mapping GHG emissions in the city. During this initial period, the partners used information provided by municipal sources to map the GHG profile of Durban and summarized current national and regional policy guidelines for climate change mitigation. In addition, the partnership found case studies of mitigation and adaptation actions that have been taken by industry partners in Durban in recent years.

In the second stage of the project, the partnership focused on communication and dialogue with stakeholders from various sectors. Communication took place in industry workshops and discussion forums that facilitated engagement among different private sector industries and exhibited current approaches to respond to climate change. The workshops included presentations on reducing carbon footprints, the use of financial mechanisms such as carbon markets and carbon credits, industrial energy efficiency and climate change strategy development.

Engagement with industry resulted in developing a generic toolkit for industrial climate change response activities. The toolkit includes baseline scenario development, a carbon footprint calculator, and tools for monitoring progress. For each sector additional elements were created:

1. A gap analysis
2. Energy management standards
3. Energy system optimization techniques
4. Tailored climate change response toolkit
5. Technology and renewable energy opportunities
6. Investment opportunities
7. Identification of specific businesses where intervention needs to take place.

The second stage also identified key industry experts and researched opportunities to attract investments from abroad. Specifically, the partnership found opportunities for Chinese investment in Durban on issues of climate change mitigation and adaptation activity.

In the final stage of the project, the partnership created an institutional mechanism that actively drives and monitors industry climate change responses in Durban. The long-term Durban Climate Change Partnership and its partnering businesses will continue to work once the project is completed to ensure that the institutional structure for applying the findings of the project is established.

The project was designed to produce four outputs.[241] The first was an agreement signed between Durban's government and local businesses to engage in climate change mitigation and adaptation processes. The second output was the signing of sector-specific compacts to reduce energy consumption and GHG emissions within specific timeframes. The compacts include learning forum models for both industry and government. The third output was the establishment of an institutional mechanism described in the third stage of the project. Finally, the fourth output established an industry forum that meets regularly to engage in a discussion on solutions for climate change mitigation and adaptation. The forum also facilitates investment and technology transfers between Durban and China.

These outputs demonstrate the structural arrangements across sectors required to limit climate change. This level of commitment does not emerge accidentally. Deliberate action leads to official agreements between government and business. Furthermore, specific industries impact climate change far greater than others. In acknowledging this reality, this partnership has encouraged new practices and secured relevant compacts. The partnership has also integrated ongoing communication and learning into its approach, as commitments, agreements, and compacts are never static. They require continuous dialogue and renewal.

WARWICKSHIRE CLIMATE CHANGE PARTNERSHIP[242]

Battling climate change has been a major part of public policy in the UK in recent years. Activity is taking place not solely on the national level; cities, counties and local communities also engage in initiatives that reduce GHG emissions and implement "green" practices. Based on the LSPs model, local climate change partnerships around the country bring together partners from the public, private, and nonprofit sector to implement innovative local solutions to the climate change debate. The Warwickshire Climate Change Partnership is one of many local partnerships in the UK that operate locally to increase the sustainability of the region and contribute to the national GHG reduction strategy.

The Warwickshire Climate Change Partnership was created under the county's LAA in alignment with the UK national energy and climate change policy. The Partnership was formed in June 2005 and officially began its operations in July 2006. It is composed of roughly 590 individuals and 200 organizations from all three sectors. As part of the Warwickshire LAA, the county committed to reaching a target of 7.2 tons of CO_2 emitted per capita in the region by 2011. This commitment translates to a reduction in per capita emissions of one ton from 2005 emissions levels.

The Partnership's website is rich with publicly available information on methodologies for promoting and implementing environmental programs in different organizations. The website offers free advice to businesses on how to improve their environmental practices. The reports offered on the website include: a handbook for reducing CO_2 emissions in small businesses, advice on recycling opportunities and on improving profitability by reducing waste and increasing energy efficiency, and an analysis of business opportunities in the region that will contribute to the transition to a low-carbon economy. In addition, the website provides community organizations and nonprofit organizations with information on opportunities for funding sustainability projects.

The Partnership works to reduce GHG emissions through engagements in five areas: energy, transport, resource efficiency, adaptation, and communication and education. In addition, the effort engages in activity on community engagement, biodiversity, horticulture and sustainable construction. There are specific programs in each area that directly target the mission of the Partnership.

Energy

The objective of the energy emphasis is to reduce GHG emissions from the use of energy by improving energy efficiency, minimizing waste, and increasing the use of renewable energy sources. The energy area is managed by the Energy Managers' Forum, which meets several times a year to discuss energy management within local public sector organizations. This objective includes several programs. The Energy Advisors program provides personalized advice to city organizations on how to reduce their environmental impact. The advisors are volunteers trained by the county. The Biomass Heating Project supports the implementation of biomass supply infrastructure and encourages organizations to conduct assessments on the feasibility of implementing biomass heating systems in their facilities. Finally, the Warwickshire Micro-wind Trial Project analyses the performance of rooftop wind turbines in the county in order to determine their financial viability.

Transport

In transportation, the Partnership's objective is to reduce GHG emissions from transport, particularly road transport, through both active programs and future transport system planning. The promotion of electric cars and buses is a key element in achieving the transport objective. Two successful programs in the transport sector are the Anti-Idling Campaign and the Biodiesel Project. The Anti-Idling Campaign is part of the Switch It Off Campaign (see Communication and Education, below). It encourages drivers to turn off idling vehicles, particularly local freight operators, to reduce their fuel consumption. The Biodiesel Project works to procure biodiesel fuel for the County Council's vehicle fleet.

Resource Efficiency

The Partnership's objective in resource management is to reduce GHG emissions through better waste management (including waste minimization), and increase recycling, more efficient use of resources, and increased use of environmentally-friendly construction. Resource efficiency programs promote the use of products that have the least impact on the environment, from their production through their use until their final disposal. Several of the programs in this area install a rainwater harvesting system in the county, the Recycled Roads Project, which reduces the amount of road aggregate waste going to landfills, and the Wolseley Sustainability Building Centre, which showcases renewable and sustainable products for construction and water conservation projects.

Adaptation

The adaptation objective of the Partnership is to minimize future risks of climate change by adopting policies and adaption measures in all organizations in the county. The Sustainability Public Buildings Project and the Public Health Services in Changing Climate initiative follow this objective.

Communication and Education

The Partnership values advocacy and education as a measure to achieving its goals. Therefore, it defined a targeted objective to communicate and educate staff and the wider community in Warwickshire on their responsibilities and actions required both to adapt to and also limit the effects of climate change in the county. Education is promoted through campaigns that increase awareness. The main program to meet this objective is the Switch It Off Campaign, which encourages public bodies, businesses, communities, schools and residents to switch off non-essential appliances when they are not needed. The campaign also implemented a Switch It Off week in 2009 that successfully increased awareness to the waste and added costs associated with plugged-in appliances when they are not used.

In 2008 the Partnership underwent a review to assess its success and identify necessary improvements. The review found that Partnership members see the building of capacity through sharing best practices the most important activity for the Partnership. Additionally, it stressed increasing efficiency and facilitating communication. Members indicated that the Partnership had been successful in obtaining robust baseline data, identifying ways to reduce fuel costs, promoting carpooling, encouraging walking and cycling, and improving waste management practices.

The range of activities pursued by this partnership demonstrates the numerous activities required to adequately address climate change. The Partnership provides a framework for how to structure a comprehensive array of programs within a specific region. These programs simultaneously encourage changed behavior within the area that can ultimately make a dent in a massive global challenge.

ENERGY AND CLIMATE CHANGE PARTNERSHIP OF THE AMERICAS – ECPA

The Energy and Climate Change Partnership of the Americas (ECPA) is a loosely organized partnership across North and South America that focuses on promoting initiatives, domestically and internationally, for energy efficiency, renewables, cleaner and more efficient use of fossil fuels, energy poverty and infrastructure.[243] ECPA was created following the invitation from President Obama in 2009 to all governments in the Western Hemisphere to collaboratively address climate change. The partnership's first year of operations resulted in the launch of numerous initiatives that address ECPA's mission. These initiatives are led by the US, Canada, Chile, Costa Rica, Mexico, Peru, and Trinidad and Tobago.

ECPA is supported by the Organization of American States, the Inter-American Development Bank, the Latin American Energy Organization, the World Bank, the private sector, civil society, academic institutions, and additional multilateral actors. In addition, state and local governments and public institutions, private sector partners and the communities involved all contribute resources to implement the initiatives. The structure of the partnership and its mission were developed at the Americas Energy and Climate Symposium that took place in June 2009 in Lima, Peru.

The partnership's various initiatives address:

- Energy efficiency: projects promote best practices through assisting the development of building codes and other standards in the industrial and residential sectors, as well as training for energy audits.
- Renewable energy: projects work to accelerate clean energy deployment via project support, policy dialogues, scientific collaboration, and creating a clean energy network.
- Cleaner and more efficient use of fossil fuels: initiatives promote

clean energy technologies to reduce conventional pollution and apply best practices for land use management.

- Energy infrastructure: projects foster modernized, integrated, and more resilient energy infrastructure, particularly electricity grids and gas pipelines.
- Energy poverty: initiatives target urban and rural energy poverty by using strategies that promote sustainable urban development and improve access to modern clean energy services and appropriate technologies in rural areas that can improve public health and reduce the use of wood for fuel.
- Sustainable forests and land use: initiatives work to reduce emissions from deforestation and forest degradation and enhance carbon sequestration, which include the conservation and sustainable management of forests.
- Adaptation: projects assist vulnerable countries and communities by providing them with strategies to understand and reduce their environmental vulnerabilities on climate change.

Current ECPA initiatives include:[244]

1. Advancing Renewables Biomass Energy
2. *Alianza entre Gulf Power – A Southern Company y el Centro de Estudios Estrategicos Latinoamericanos* (CEELAT)
3. Central American Energy and Environmental Security Initiative (EESI)
4. *Centro de Energia Renovable de Chile*
5. *Centro de Innovacion Energetica*
6. Chile Renewable Energy Center
7. Closed-Looped Cycle Production in Ecuador
8. Colombia Biomass Initiative
9. *Comunidades de las Americas con Baja Emision de Carbono: Centro Costarricense de Capacitacion sobre Eficienca Energetica*
10. *Comunidades de las Americas con Baja Emision de Carbono: Proyecto Eolico de Dominica*
11. *Comunidades del Caribe con Baja Emision de Carbono* (LCCC)
12. ECPA Caribbean Initiative
13. Energy Efficiency Working Group
14. Energy Innovation Center
15. Global Shale Gas Initiative: South America
16. *Grupo de Trabajo en Eficiencia Energetica*
17. *Grupo de Trabajo sobre Infraestructura Energetica – Interconexion Electrica*

18. *Grupo de Trabajo sobre Petroleo Pesado*
19. Heavy Oil Working Group
20. *Iluinando las Americas*
21. *Iniciativa Centroamericana de Energia y Seguridad Ambiental* (EESI)
22. *Inciativa de Biomasa de Colombia*
23. *Inciativa de la ECPA para el Caribe*
24. *Inciativa de planificacion urbana*
25. *Inciativa Global de Gas de Esquisto: Sudamerica*
26. *Inciativa sobre Energia Renovable y Cambio Climatico del del Cuerpo de Paz*
27. Lighting the Americas
28. Low Carbon Communities of the Americas (LCCA): Dominica Wind Project
29. Partnership between Gulf Power – A Southern Company and *Centro de Estudios Estrategicos Latinoamericanos* (CEELAT)
30. Peace Corps Renewable Energy and Climate Change Initiative
31. *Produccion en Ciclo Cerrado en Ecuador*
32. *Programa de Expertos ee la biomasa*
33. Senior ECPA Fellows Program
34. Urban Planning Initiative
35. USTDA – *Programa de Intercambio de Energia no Contaminante de las Americas*
36. USTDA Clean Energy Exchange Program of the Americas.

Examples of leading initiatives are detailed below.

Central American Energy and Environmental Security Initiative (EESI)[245]

The goal of the Central American Energy and Environmental Security Initiative (EESI) is to accelerate the deployment of clean energy, promote energy efficiency, and increase energy security by helping Central America move from plan to action on climate change adaptation. The initiative supports activities to accelerate its mission in coordination with Central American governments. EESI organizes workshops, seminars and other capacity building events to educate regulators and legislators on the advantages of clean energy and smart grid development. EESI also supports smart grid pilot projects in Costa Rica that are jointly implemented by private sector partners. The initiative is financed and implemented by the US Department of State.

Chile Renewable Energy Centers[246]

The US Department of Energy is providing technical assistance to develop Regional Clean Energy Centers throughout the hemisphere by gathering and disseminating data and best practices on clean energy technology and research and development. The Chilean center serves as an information hub; it includes analytical tools and expertise on renewable energy technologies and policies. The centers help research, develop and promote nonconventional renewable energy projects. The initiative's implementing partners are *Corporación de Fomento de la Producción de Chile* (CORFO), *Centro de Energias Renovables* (CER), *Gobierno de Chile*, Inter-American Development Bank (IDB), National Renewable Energy Laboratory (NREL), and the US Department of Energy. The financing partners are the Chilean Ministry of Energy, the US Department of Energy, and the IDB.

ECPA Caribbean Initiative[247]

The ECPA Caribbean Initiative promotes sustainable energy policies and programs that assist governments to deploy renewable energy projects by providing short-term legal counsel and technical assistance to clean energy projects. Antigua and Barbuda, Bahamas, Barbados, Belize, Dominica, Dominican Republic, Grenada, Guyana, Haiti, Jamaica, Saint Kitts and Nevis, Saint Lucia, Saint Vincent and the Grenadines, Suriname, and Trinidad and Tobago all participate in this initiative. Managed by the Organization of American States' Department of Sustainable Development, the program helps Caribbean governments promote and implement sustainable energy policies and programs. The initiative supports regional dialogue among Caribbean energy ministers, donor governments, regional multilateral institutions and civil society to explore long-term energy security solutions. The initiative also provides technical and legal assistance, as well as fostering partnerships between governments and university research partners. The initiative is funded by the US Department of State.

Lighting the Americas[248]

The US Department of State is working with the governments of Brazil, Chile and Peru to provide grid access to the 34 million people in Latin America still without access to electricity. The grid extensions are supplemented by PV and mini-hydro systems. Current assessments state that the overall cost of providing grid access to rural communities in

Latin America could reach $2 billion over ten years. The initiative receives financial support from the IDB.

Peace Corps Renewable Energy and Climate Change Initiative[249]

This initiative focuses on educating communities on climate change, energy efficiency, renewable energy, and mitigation and adaptation to climate change. The Peace Corps project also supports community efforts to secure micro-loans to implement and access renewable energy technologies. Countries participating in this initiative include Costa Rica, the Dominican Republic, El Salvador, Guatemala, Guyana, Honduras, Nicaragua, Panama, Paraguay, Peru, and Suriname. The US Qualified Peace Corps members train municipal staff and community members on climate change, natural resource management, energy efficiency, and renewable energy technologies, as well as adaptation to and mitigation of climate change. Peace Corps volunteers support community projects, such as solar or fuel efficient stoves and ovens, bio-digesters for household cooking, solar water heating, solar panels for electricity, wind power generation, and more. Peace Corps volunteers also train and support microfinance institutions to create systems that provide funding for renewable energy and climate change technologies. In each country, Peace Corps volunteers work with host governments, international, national and local partners to facilitate projects and improve access to energy and income-generating opportunities. The Peace Corps and US Department of State both implement and finance the initiative.

USTDA Clean Energy Exchange Program of the Americas[250]

The US Trade and Development Agency (USTDA) Clean Energy Exchange Program of the Americas brings nearly 50 Latin American and Caribbean energy officials and project sponsors to the US for a series of six reverse trade missions. Each mission includes clean energy site visits and meetings with US agencies, US industry companies and financial institutions. The meetings allow for the sharing of information on the commercial, technological, regulatory, and financial aspects of clean energy project development. The reverse missions each focus on one specific clean energy issue or technology. USTDA anticipates that the Clean Energy Exchange Program will foster future projects and collaboration opportunities for both the private and public sector. The USTDA is implementing and financing the initiative.

Overall, the climate change challenge is all-consuming, touching all aspects of society and every corner of the globe. It requires changed behavior across the board. Any challenge of this magnitude can only be addressed through intentional cooperation across sectors and industries.

11. Improving global health

Health disparities and vast differences in access to health care are among the great challenges of our times. Aligning health-oriented companies (pharmaceutical firms), health policy, hospitals and clinics, and various NGOs working directly with disenfranchised populations can begin to create greater equity in health and health care.

The 1978 Declaration of Alma-Ata, the first international declaration of its kind, proclaimed primary health care a "fundamental human right" and the attainment of the highest possible level of health "a most important world-wide social goal." It has since been widely accepted that the promotion of health is essential to sustaining economic and social development as well as to contributing to world peace.

And yet, despite progress in nations such as Brazil, Chile, China, Mexico, Rwanda, and Thailand,[251] the world is not yet positioned to ensure the level of health care access that the signatories of the 1978 Declaration envisioned. According to the WHO's 2010 World Health Report, citing the International Labour Organization, only one in five people in the world has social security protection broad enough to cover for lost wages in the event of illness, while more than half of the world's population lacks formal social protection. In sub-Saharan Africa and Southern Asia, the coverage rate is as low as 5–10 percent. In middle-income countries, between 20 percent and 60 percent are covered.[252] Faced with rising costs and demographic changes, high-income countries cannot be complacent. Germany, for example, has recognized that it can no longer rely solely on traditional sources of wage-based insurance contributions with its aging population and has allocated additional funds from general revenues into its social health system.[253]

In its 2002 World Health Report, the WHO has identified ten leading risk factors accounting for a vast number of premature deaths and a large percentage of the global burden of disease: underweight, unsafe sex, high blood pressure, tobacco consumption, alcohol consumption, unsafe water, sanitation and hygiene, iron deficiency, indoor smoke from solid fuels, high cholesterol, and obesity. More than a third of all deaths worldwide are results of these ten risk factors.[254] Intervention from public, private, and nongovernmental actors can limit these risk factors and their effects.

SALUD MESOAMÉRICA 2015

The Salud Mesoamérica 2015 (SM2015)[255] initiative was launched in June 2010. The initiative brings together the Bill & Melinda Gates Foundation, the Carlos Slim Health Institute, the government of Spain, and the IDB around a common agenda.[256] It was created to reduce the health equity gaps that disadvantage individuals living in extreme poverty in Mesoamerica. This five-year endeavor is scheduled to end in 2015.

Countries involved in the initiative include Belize, Costa Rica, El Salvador, Guatemala, Honduras, Nicaragua, Panama, and nine states in Southern Mexico. The mission of the partnership is to back the efforts of Mesoamerican governments in reaching the health MDGs through investments in projects with proven success for the poorest 20 percent of the population in this region, and in particular women and children under five years old.

The partnership operates according to seven principles:[257]

1. A focus on health equity for those living in extreme poverty
2. Country ownership of projects that must also align with national and regional policies
3. Impact and results-based focus
4. Performance management and evaluation
5. Transparency and accountability
6. "Additionality", meaning that the partnership's financing cannot replace national financing
7. Coordination and collaboration with regional agencies.

The partnership expands health coverage and increases the quality and use of basic public health services in the areas of reproductive, maternal, neonatal and child health care, maternal and child nutrition, immunization, malaria and dengue, with long-term goals to:

1. Increase the availability and use of evidence to formulate pro-poor health policies
2. Create a long-term political and financial commitment to close the health equity gap in the region
3. Increase the supply, quality and use of basic health services in poor communities
4. Contribute to the elimination of malaria and the control of dengue.

Based on a preliminary costing study[258] for the seven countries of Mesoamerica and Mexico, an approximate investment of $564 million over five years will be needed to close the coverage gap for basic health services between the poorest 20 percent of these populations and the national averages. The SM2015 funding will not entirely cover the gap; thus, the initiative also includes a resource mobilization strategy to seek private and public partnerships that will complement and contribute to the main components of the initiative.[259]

The Initiative is guided by the unique logic model and the SM2015 Theory of Change, two conceptual frameworks which illustrate the rationale for strategic planning, decision-making processes and evaluation as methods for reaching a specific goal. The SM2015 Theory of Change promotes a "Results-Based Financing" (RBF) model. This approach provides economic incentives to national-level health providers and encourages local innovative results. Health providers, households, health systems, donors, and policy makers are all essential actors in SM2015. The initiative sees the Mesoamerican region's maternal and child health and nutrition as resulting from the interface between households and health providers. Public resources that can shape the capacity of health institutions and assist families are determined by policy allocations. At times, grants from donors fuel these public budgets. SM2015 hopes to align incentives for this range of stakeholders to improve the quality of and access to health care.[260]

The partnership's operating model focuses on both the supply and demand of basic health services. The Bill & Melinda Gates Foundation, the Carlos Slim Health Institute and the government of Spain each contributed $50 million towards the partnership's programs, while IDB serves as the program's implementing agency. IDB is responsible for designing the projects with each country's ministry of health, as well as helping the governments improve their information systems and strengthen their human capital. SM2015 will work with regional entities like the Mesoamerican Public Health System (SMSP) and the Council of Central American Health Ministers (COMISCA) to coordinate health service improvement efforts while also building capacity (through lessons learned and firsthand experience) for possible future replication efforts.

Country-level activities for SM2015 include evidence-based health interventions that have been proven to reduce morbidity and mortality in women of reproductive age and children; interventions are conceived as a set of integrated actions provided along the life cycle (pre-conception through early childhood). Interventions are to occur in the course of two to three 18-month operations in each country. The partnership has implemented its RBF model in which all funds provided by the initiative are matched by the host country to finance program operations. In this model, a portion of the funding is disbursed after governments reach their targets for broadening coverage, improving the quality of health services, and adopting evidence-based technical and fiscal health policies. Targets are measured independently from time to time for disbursement of the performance portion of the funding. This model provides for three tranches of funding at the country level: an initial grant or investment tranche, country counterpart funding, and a performance tranche.

The country is guaranteed the first tranche if it contributes the counterpart funds (equal to 50 percent, on average, of the project budget for all operations); together, these funds create the project budget. It can only spend these funds upon the implementation of evidence-based health interventions. The performance tranche is equal to 50 percent of the counterpart funding and is disbursed in the event that the results initially set for each operation are achieved; these funds must then be used for public health purposes. This financing model increases the incentives for the country to effectively create and manage the programs it launches. As of December 2011, the governments of four SM2015 countries – Honduras, Nicaragua, Mexico, Belize – had opted to replicate the RBF model, extending it downward for application at the state and local levels.[261]

The partnership is based on monitoring and assessment principles. All programs are subject to periodic evaluations to ensure they are reaching their goals. The partnership conducts an initial assessment in each country to determine the baseline health service coverage (measured according to 10–12 indicators for each country), and then follow-up surveys every 18–24 months, which are used to direct national policy dialogues and inform future projects. SM2015 monitoring and evaluation includes establishing baselines for performance tracking; developing regular, timely systems for collecting data directly from different levels of the project; designing regional, national and sub-national scorecards for tracking progress; improving the capacity of participants to use evidence in decision-making; and standardizing data collection and reporting in the region. The monitoring of progress and the RBF model together provide rigorous checks on the quality of service and align incentives for improving health impacts. In addition, emphasizing the importance of measuring program impacts increases transparency and accountability towards the communities, civil society institutions in the region, and donors.

The partnership works in three principle areas – nutrition, immunizations, and maternal, child, and reproductive health. In the area of nutrition, the partnership is implementing programs that increase consumption through Conditional Cash Transfers and others that provide complementary fortified foods and micronutrients. Regarding immunizations, the partnership focuses on closing information gaps, strengthening immunization policies, and implementing evidence-based best practices. To improve maternal, child health and reproductive health care, the partnership is implementing better service practices, particularly for newborns, and wishes to inform the population on at least six methods for family planning.

The partnership expects the following results:

- Significant reduction in under-five child mortality rates
- Reduction in chronic malnutrition and micronutrient deficiencies in children aged under 24 months and pregnant women
- An increase in the rates and quality of child immunization in poor regions
- Increase in the coverage and quality of prenatal and postnatal care and access to family planning
- More emphasis on data collection and evidence for formulating health policies designed for people living in extreme poverty
- Measurement and evaluation of the performance of all of the initiative's operations
- Reduction in the transmission of malaria
- A reduction of dengue vectors and improvement of diagnosis, care, and timely notification of dengue cases.

As of December 2011, seven out of eight country-level operations had been prepared (in El Salvador, Guatemala, Belize, Panama, and Nicaragua); five of those seven were to be approved by the project partners by December 16, 2011. The remaining three country-level operations were to be prepared and approved by March 2012. Operation plans are contracts – signed and legally binding – between the IDB and the participating governments, and include operation objectives, strategy, and measurement indicators. For countries with approved operation plans, the first disbursements were to be made between January and March 2012; El Salvador was to receive the first disbursement.

According to Dr. Emma Margarita Iriarte, Principal Coordinator for SM2015, one of the most significant challenges thus far has been introducing the results-based implementation model at the country level. Most health ministry employees are used to projects measured by "budget lines:" for such projects, the success of implementation is measured by the number of services successfully delivered. In the case of SM2015, each country must monitor and implement with the aim of achieving results (not just executing activities), but introducing this "paradigm shift" at the health ministry level has been challenging.[262]

Clear, measurable results elude many partnerships. SM2015's highly organized design builds in evaluation mechanisms from the beginning, establishing baseline data and continually assessing progress. Its creative financing model leverages public and private funding tied to demonstrable advances. Anticipated results around child mortality, immunization, and prenatal care represent a focused attempt to address health concerns in multiple countries early in life.

THE ACCESS PROJECT

The Access Project[263] (the Project) brings together institutions from the public, private and nonprofit sectors to improve the health of impoverished people, communities and countries. It applies private sector and management practices to public health systems in developing countries meant to increase access to life-saving drugs and health services. The partnership offers technical assistance, facilitates targeted financial planning, and provides in-depth training to health centers' managers to ensure the effectiveness and transparency of their operations. Upon improving their services and processes, centers become eligible for international funding sources, such as the Global Fund. Currently, the Access Project is active primarily in Rwanda, where it began its operations.

The Project views public health as a development issue; a healthy population is more productive and has better opportunities to exit poverty. At health centers, the Project encounters management deficiencies (financial, human resources, drug procurement), understaffing, and insufficient infrastructure such as water and electricity. The Project's mission is carried out through strategic partnerships with the Rwandan Ministry of Health, NGOs operating in the region, private foundations, universities, official government aid agencies, corporations, small businesses, community health workers, health care staff, and the communities that are being served.[264] The partnership's major private funders include The Glaser Progress Foundation, MAC AIDS Fund, the Schmidt Family Foundation, the MAIA Foundation, Legatum Group, and the Garth Brooks Teammates for Kids Foundation.

The partnership works in eight management domains:

1. Human resources
2. Infrastructure
3. Finance

4. Community health insurance
5. Pharmacy logistics
6. Health information systems
7. Planning and coordination
8. Information technology.

Technical experts with the help of local health administrators implement each system. The systems are personally designed to work with the constraints faced by many Rwandan health centers. These constraints include the lack of uninterrupted power supply or health care workers with limited education. The Access Project currently focuses on three major initiatives – improving health management in Rwanda, developing health-related infrastructure, and controlling neglected tropical diseases.

Advancing Health Management

As part of its efforts to improve the management of health services in Rwanda, the Access Project developed the Access Management Evaluation Tool, a quantitative measure for assessing management operations. The Project applies the tool to measure the performance of health center management and provide the leadership of health centers with guidelines for improvement. The partnership also offers mentoring services and trainings provided by district-based advisors. Since 2006, the Project's operations expanded from three to six regions. Today the Project works with 79 health centers servicing close to two million people. The evaluation tool is used periodically to assess the development and continuous operations of health centers in Rwanda.

Developing Health Infrastructure

The Access Project works to ensure that health centers have access to clean water, electricity and all other forms of critical infrastructure required to provide effective health services. Where vital infrastructure is lacking, the Access Project partners with Rwanda Works to raise the funds needed for major health care construction projects. Rwanda Works is an NGO devoted to improving health and creating prosperity. This partnership is responsible for the construction of three new health centers in Rwanda. All three centers are located in Bugesera, one of the country's poorest districts that was also most affected by the 1994 genocide. The Ministry of Health has committed to equipping and staffing these and any additional new centers constructed by the Access Project.

The Project's goal is to construct 17 new facilities that will service over 300,000 individuals who do not have access to a health center and reside in the six operational districts. Each health center requires contribution and investment from many partners; the local community donates land and manual labor, the national government provides investment to train staff and fund operating costs, and local and international donors pay for construction, design and other skilled labor. Each construction project costs between $500,000 and $700,000. As of early 2009, the Access Project secured close to $2 million in contributions from private donors for health center construction.

Controlling Neglected Tropical Diseases

In 2007, the Access Project launched Rwanda's first Neglected Tropical Diseases (NTD) Control Program in partnership with the Rwandan Ministry of Health. The NTDs battled in the country are trachoma, schistosomiasis and intestinal worms, all of which are treatable and preventable. The program was spearheaded by mapping NTDs in the country. The mapping project guides interventions, primarily twice-yearly administration of related drugs to most children in the country. The mapping initiative was funded by Geneva Global through the Sabine Vaccine Institute. It measured the distribution, prevalence, and intensity of four NTDs that are most likely to negatively affect the population of Rwanda – soil transmitted helminth infections (also known as intestinal worms), schistosomiasis, trachoma, and lymphatic filariasis. The mapping revealed:

1.   Intestinal worms are prevalent among 66 percent of school-aged children, posing a major public health issue.
2.   Schistosomiasis, while affecting few Rwandan children overall, affects 70 percent of schoolchildren living near lakes or swamps.
3.   Trachoma, an eye infection that can lead to blindness, is not a major public health issue in Rwanda.
4.   Lymphatic filariasis, also known as elephantiasis, is not prevalent in any part of the country.

The mapping initiative also showed that NTDs flourish in poor communities where sanitation, water conditions, and dilapidated housing are prevalent.

In addition to the mapping initiative, the Rwandan NTD program trained 230 lab technicians to diagnose critical NTDs, and equipped their labs with the necessary equipment in areas with high NTD infection rates. The program also trained 13 medical doctors, 16 ophthalmological health workers, 3439 primary school teachers, 10,288 community health workers, 707 health workers and 108 local authority officers and journalists in identifying, preventing and treating intestinal worms and schistosomiasis. In addition, the program administered two rounds of preventative chemotherapy to four million adults and children in Rwanda. Finally, the program developed and launched a mass media education campaign to increase awareness of NTDs.

The NTD program is already showing positive results. An impact assessment demonstrated that awareness for NTDs is high among government employees, the health care community, and vulnerable adults and children. In addition, in areas where the Access Project and its partners conducted interventions, the infection rate was lower than prior to the intervention. The Project is now refocusing on long-term strategies that will help patients infected by NTDs to manage their long-term care and prevent possible disability and death as a result of NTDs.

The Access Project is implanting the range of services required to address health challenges in an area with limited health infrastructure. In order to achieve this mission, the Project has facilitated collaboration across various partners across sectors. The Project has been increasing the capacity of health centers, and addresses critical infrastructure challenges in order to provide an environment conducive to routinely providing adequate health care. Its mapping efforts have revealed important data to guide health interventions. Overall, this effort's experiences illustrate what is possible when the proper resources are coordinated to target health needs in an environment that lacks the adequate health care infrastructure in an impoverished environment.

The Project's results show increased awareness and decreased infection rates. But they also highlight the magnitude of the challenge ahead – to establish permanent infrastructures that can limit the effects of NTDs. The need for resources to support comprehensive health care provision always remains. In its formative phase of development, the Access Project has made measurable progress, and laid the groundwork for longer-term improved health in Rwanda.

PFIZER TRACHOMA INITIATIVE

Another partnership addressing NTD is the Pfizer Trachoma Initiative[265] – a collaborative effort between Pfizer, the International Trachoma Initiative (ITI) and the World Health Organization's Alliance for the

Global Elimination of Blinding Trachoma. The program's goal is to "end the suffering and the cycle of poverty" caused by trachoma by 2020.[266]

Trachoma is a treatable, infectious disease that spreads through contact with an infected person's hands or clothing. About 41 million people, mostly women and children, in 57 countries have active trachoma infection and need treatment.[267] Children are very susceptible to infections. However, blindness does not occur until adulthood. The disease tends to disproportionally affect the poorest of the poor, who also suffer from limited access to water and sanitation. Since trachoma is transmitted through physical contact, it often infects whole families or communities. Pfizer estimates that 1.2 billion people live in trachoma-endemic areas.

ITI was created in 1998 by the Edna McConnell Clark Foundation and Pfizer with the mission of eliminating blinding trachoma. ITI manages Pfizer's global donation of the antibiotic Zithromax, the primary contribution of Pfizer to the Trachoma Initiative. ITI also collaborates with governmental and nongovernmental agencies on the local, national and international levels to implement treatment strategies.

The Pfizer Trachoma Initiative partners with the Bill & Melinda Gates Foundation, the Carter Center, CBM (formerly known as Christian Blind Mission), Helen Keller International, Lions Club International, Sight Savers International, The US Fund for UNICEF, World Health Organization, governments, NGOs, corporations, UN agencies and others.

As of September 2011, the initiative has achieved the following:

1.   The program donated more than 225 million doses of Zithromax treatments to people in 19 countries and supported the performance of surgeries to treat advanced cases of trachoma. The support totaled $5 billion.
2.   With the support of the program, ITI, and work done by other partners, in 2006 Morocco became the first country to eliminate trachoma.
3.   With the assistance of the trachoma initiative, Gambia, Ghana and Vietnam are on track to eliminating blinding trachoma.

In Vietnam, the program has been particularly successful and is on track to eliminating trachoma. In 2007 trachoma was no longer considered a public health problem when the infection rate fell below 5 percent.[268] ITI began working in Vietnam in 2000. Since then, 83,830 Vietnamese have undergone surgery to save their vision from blindness. In addition, Pfizer donated over 2.1 million doses of Zithromax in Vietnam. The success of the program is coupled with education on sanitation and hygiene, primarily among children. School programs that promote facial washing and water sanitation have been successful in increasing awareness for cleanliness and, as a result, have helped to slow the infection rates of trachoma in the country. Pfizer has embarked on a mutually beneficial strategy to spread the use of Zithromax and cure a treatable disease by collaborating with various partners who bring relevant resources and expertise. This partnership exemplifies how a purposeful cross sector partnership can achieve demonstrable results. The initiative's goals are clear. Its methods are feasible, and ultimately successful.

This effort is a compelling example of how a major corporation such as Pfizer can fulfil its self-interest, by increasing the use of one of its products, Zithromax, while meeting a broad public need in multiple nations. All of these health partnerships crystallize what it takes to provide adequate health interventions for populations susceptible to treatable diseases, but lacking access to adequate care. It is difficult to imagine how the populations that have benefitted from the activities of these partnerships could have received the level of care or medicine without comprehensive cross sector collaboration. The cooperation of local governments, the resources of the private sector, the commitment of NGOs with health missions, and the increased capacity of local health institutions and providers all contribute to the level of required intervention.

12. Addressing poverty

According to the World Bank, people in developing countries living on less than $1.25 – the international poverty line – has decreased from 1.9 billion people in 1990 to 1.29 billion in 2008. In percentage terms, this means a decline from 43 percent of the population in 1990 to 22.4 percent in 2008.[269] In the industrialized countries, inequality has been on the rise. According to the 2011 OECD report, "Divided We Stand: Why Inequality Keeps Rising," real disposable household incomes increased by an average of 1.7 percent per year in OECD countries over the two decades preceding the onset of the global economic crisis. However, in a large majority of these countries, the household incomes of the richest 10 percent grew faster than those of the poorest 10 percent, exacerbating the income gap.

In Japan, the real incomes of those at the bottom of the income ladder have declined since the mid-1980s. Moreover, the richest 10 percent in OECD countries today dispose of an average income about nine times higher than that of the poorest 10 percent, or a ratio of 9:1. However, this ratio is not uniform across OECD countries. While the Nordic and many of the continental European countries enjoy a much lower ratio than the 9:1 OECD average, Italy, Japan, Korea, and the UK have a ratio of 10:1. In Israel, Turkey, and the US, the ratio is around 14:1, while in Mexico and Chile, it is 27:1.[270]

In the emerging economies of Argentina, Brazil, China, India, Indonesia, the Russian Federation, and South Africa, income inequality is significantly higher than the OECD average. While Brazil, Indonesia, and Argentina have improved significantly in this realm according to some indicators over the past 20 years, inequality has increased in China, India, the Russian Federation, and South Africa over time.[271]

In the US, according to the latest available Census Report, "Income, Poverty, and Health Insurance Coverage in the United States: 2010,"[272] the poverty rate in 2010 – the first full calendar year after the end of the recession in June 2009 – was 15.1 percent, which is the highest rate since 1993. Up from the 14.3 percent rate in 2009, the 2010 figure is the third consecutive annual increase in poverty rate, totaling a 2.6 percent increase since 2007. The 46.2 million people in poverty in 2010 represent the largest number in the 52 years for which poverty estimates have been published.[273]

Poverty cuts across all social concerns. Any poverty reduction attempt must be comprehensive, focused, and sufficiently financed. Because of poverty's extensive and pervasive effects, strategies to change the circumstances of impoverished populations are inherently multi-issue. Poverty encompasses education, health, economic development, and a number of critical issues. The life circumstances of impoverished communities cannot change with limited or short-term approaches. The depth of the challenge facing these populations calls for substantial protracted commitment across sectors.

MILLENNIUM PROMISE/MILLENNIUM VILLAGES PROJECT

The Millennium Promise[274] is an example of one such attempt to draw upon the resources and expertise of multiple stakeholders across sectors to transform select impoverished communities. This nonprofit organization, established in 2005, works to achieve the MDGs. The organization launched the Millennium Villages Project (MVP) in 2006 to apply the principles of the MDGs into action. The MVP primarily addresses the first MDG – to end poverty and hunger.[275] The initiative brings together actors from all sectors that work together to fund and help with the operations of "Millennium Villages" (MVs). Fourteen MV sites in ten countries in sub-Saharan Africa have been created. The MVP affects the lives of over 500,000 people and intends to expand its operations in the next several years.

The MVP's primary partners include Columbia University's Earth Institute, Millennium Promise, the United Nations, and the host governments: Ethiopia, Ghana, Kenya, Malawi, Mali, Nigeria, Rwanda, Senegal, Tanzania, and Uganda. The Earth Institute provides research and expertise on the development of science-based solutions for the MVP. Millennium Promise raises funds, works with partner organizations to support the project, and engages with the private sector to develop markets around the villages. The UN agencies involved provide project management and operational support, in addition to human resources services in Africa. The UNDP is currently also working on scaling up MVP activities to the national level. In addition, many other partners from the private, public, academic and nonprofit sectors contribute in many ways to the operations of the MVs.[276]

The MVs manage programs on several critical issues – agriculture, education, health, infrastructure and energy, water and sanitation, environment, gender equality, and community development and local governance.

Agriculture

The MVs' agricultural approach expands economic activity by developing business opportunities for farmers. Farmers seek opportunities to develop their businesses through crop diversification and cooperative formation. The MVP provides farmers with technical support that helps them focus on speciality crops and value chains, assistance in accessing finance, and workshops and educational tools to help farmers improve their operational techniques. Several successful businesses, like the cassava bakery in Mwandama (Malawi) and the onion cooperatives in Potou (Senegal), have already started operating.

Agriculture businesses in the MVs are slowly reducing dependence on subsidy programs while increasing the use of credit-based financing. The funds are primarily used for acquisition of fertilizer and other agricultural inputs. The MVP notes that repayment of credit is more successful when the finance is provided by external lending institutions rather than the MVP itself.

Education

The MVP manages several educational initiatives in the villages. In 2010, the MVP focused on expanding the school meal program, providing more information technology in classrooms, and increasing access to secondary education. In order to increase the school meal program's sustainability, the MVP partners with the foundation Table for Two and the World Food Programme. Additionally, part of the MV harvest is apportioned to the school meal program, and on-site gardens in some schools complement current capacity.

The MVs expanded and upgraded technology in classrooms. In 2010 Lenovo donated almost 200 computers to MVs. As a result, all MV classrooms now have between four and 26 computers. In order to increase access to secondary education, the MVP and Millennium Promise Japan provide scholarships to students to attend secondary school, focusing on girls. The MVP provides several elements that complement education services in the villages: free learning materials, tutoring sessions for struggling students, teacher training, and community-led school enrolment drives. Some MVs in rural areas struggle to find qualified teachers. To overcome this challenge, the MVs offer incentives to teachers such as health care, housing, fertilizer or bank loans. This combination of interventions on education has helped increase student enrolment and performance in MVs. For example, in Mbola, school attendance rates increased from 60 percent in 2006 to 96 percent in 2010; enrolment rates increased from 70 percent in 2006 to 96 percent in 2010.

Health

The MVP advances several initiatives to improve the health of MV residents. Today all 14 MV sites offer free health care. One of the signature programs in the villages is the Community Health Worker (CHW) System – a network of health care workers trained by the MVP providing services to families and communities living in rural and remote areas. The CHW System operates with mobile health technology, including mobile texting for health record-keeping. The MVP is now addressing the compensation problem with CHWs in order to transition them from volunteers to employees. The MVP health teams also began offering resuscitation training for newborn babies to health workers in 2010.

ICT is becoming an indispensable component of health care provision in MVs. The ChildCount+ system uses mobile messaging to facilitate and coordinate health care workers' activities in the MVs. The text messages register patients and report their health status to a central web dashboard that provides a comprehensive view on the health of the community. The system was rolled out to all MV sites after being tested in Sauri.

The MVs are still struggling with a few challenges on health issues. Several sites are missing essential components such as piped water or critical maternity centers. In addition, MV health centers are often strained due to poor management of supply chains and high capacity of patients that arrive from outside the MV jurisdiction area.

Infrastructure and Energy

One of the MVP's main goals is to increase the access of MVs to infrastructure. By the end of 2010 most of the roads planned by the MVP had been completed. In addition, projects to extend the electricity grid had major breakthroughs that year. Teams are now working to transfer the responsibility for maintaining the new roads, water systems and buildings to the local governments.

The MVP is developing solar micro-grid systems that can serve areas too distant from the main grid to receive services. The SharedSolar initiative is a pay-as-you-go system that meets the needs of rural villages by offering low initial costs and administrative burdens, high reliability and on-demand power almost 24 hours a day. SharedSolar is being installed in Tiby, Mbola, and Ruhiira. The MVP Lantern Program provides technology for lighting and power for cell phone charging for off-grid homes and businesses. After a pilot in Mwandama where nearly 1000 lanterns were sold, the program was implemented in ten MVs. Despite advances in micro-grid technology, the current available solutions are not appropriate for all clients, leaving room for the development of new technologies.

Eleven MVs launched the Cook Stove Program in 2010. The stoves are energy efficient and compatible with traditional cooking preferences. The program includes pilot testing, vendor training, and strengthening co-operatives. By coordinating the bulk procurement of solar panels, lanterns and stoves, the MVP is able to keep prices low for consumers.

Water and Sanitation

The MVP goal on water and sanitation is to provide all MV residents access to 20 liters of improved water per day from a water point within 500 meters from their households that serves no more than 400 people, and access to an improved sanitation facility, usually in the form of a latrine, no more than 50 meters away. Most MVs are on track to meet this goal. The MVP's interventions on water and sanitation included increasing access to improved water sources through the installation of more wells and pumps close to households, schools, health clinics, and markets; rehabilitating broken boreholes and pumps; promoting the protection of springs; and continuing to develop piped water systems in villages. JM Eagle, a PVC manufacturer that has been a great supporter of the MVP water and sanitation initiatives, had provided nearly 335 miles of pipes for water systems to eight MVs by 2010.

One of the challenges faced by MVs is maintaining the cleanliness of local water sources. To overcome the challenge, the MVP promotes public awareness about spring protection and the use of latrines. The MVP also distributes water treatment tablets and water purification sachets where the challenge is greatest.

Environment

The MVP defined three goals for the environment:

1. To reverse deforestation and desertification
2. To mitigate climate change
3. To promote sustainable agricultural practices that promote bio-diversity.

The MVP developed multiple initiatives to address these goals. The MVP implemented the Integrated Soil Fertility Management (ISFM), which increases crop yields. ISFM rehabilitates the organic matter in soil and can complement or replace mineral fertilizers. In addition, all MVs include reforestation activities, such as training sessions in nursery management, production of high-yield agro-forestry trees, and out-planting seedlings in degraded common land. Several of the MVs are also implementing erosion structures to limit sand transport. To encourage participation in environmental programs that often have more long-term benefits than other interventions, the MVP launched a carbon credit pilot program to provide financial incentives to participate in agro-forestry and ISFM programs.

Environmental interventions are informed by science and research provided by the Earth Institute's Tropical Agriculture and Rural Environment Program. The Program examines the interactions between agriculture production, environmental quality and human wellbeing. The World Agro-forestry Center (ICRAF) provides environmental assessments of all MVP sites.

Gender Equality

The MVP works diligently to promote gender equality. On the community level, MVP workers conduct workshops for parents, educators, and school management committees to address issues of gender-based violence, sexual and reproductive health, and the importance of educating girls. To improve gender equality in schools, the MVs initiate girls' empowerment clubs, promote girl-friendly environments, and run mentoring and tutoring programs. Connect to Learn is a program that provides scholarships to students that cannot afford their education, particularly for girls. The MVs facilitate the development of female empowerment groups that help women find access to social and financial support. In addition, infrastructure activities in MVs, such as bringing water sources closer to households, are informed by gender equality issues.

Community Development and Local Governance

Since 2006, all MVs have facilitated the development of Community Action Plans (CAPs), which document a shared work plan geared towards achieving the MDGs. In several MVs, the MVP assists in strengthening relationships between the villages and local leaders. The MVP is beginning to transfer the management of MV projects to local bodies. In addition, the MV site teams are implementing interventions that are meant to improve the performance of sub-district governments in order to overcome the insufficient capacity of local governments to take full ownership over MV activity.

Measuring Success

The MVP instituted comprehensive assessments to measures its success rates. The MVP is evaluated quarterly based on 87 performance indicators, which are recorded in an off-site central information system. Health data is recorded in several ways. Vital Events Monitoring keeps track of all births and deaths using cell phone technology. Several MVs also introduced an electronic medical record system.

The MVP undergoes a comprehensive evaluation every three years. In these evaluations the MVP administers 40,000 questionnaires to residents of MVs and collects 25,000 biological specimens and other measurements. The first report, entitled "Harvests of Development in Rural Africa", documented several positive findings for the first three years of the project. During this period:

1. Maize crop yields almost tripled on average across all villages
2. Chronic malnutrition decreased by 30 percent among children under two years old
3. There was a reduction of almost 60 percent in malaria prevalence, in part due to increased bed net use
4. More than 80 percent of children receive school meals
5. Forty percent more women gave birth with skilled birth attendants
6. Access to water sources increased more than threefold and access to sanitation facilities increased almost sevenfold.

As a result of these findings, the MVP prioritized four countries that will receive special focus for the next stage of the project. These countries are Ghana, Mali, Kenya, and Malawi. In these countries, the MVP will develop cooperatives by supporting the writing of business plans, the development of business skills among local managers and entrepreneurs, fostering value chain management, attracting local service providers, and fine-tuning business development interventions and systems.

The MVP has taken a compelling approach to leveraging resources from various parties across sectors to address the range of issues in the MDGs, and beyond, in specific African communities. The experience of this initiative illustrates the magnitude of the challenges confronting impoverished communities. The MVP's broad network of researchers, scientists, corporations, private investors, and local governments comprises a unique model to address poverty reduction. The effort has integrated a multifaceted evaluation to measure progress. Progress to date is noticeable, but the challenge of any partnership with numerous goals around the extensive effects of poverty is to sustain progress over the long run.

THE SOUTHERN AGRICULTURAL GROWTH CORRIDOR OF TANZANIA (SAGCOT)

The Southern Agricultural Growth Corridor of Tanzania (SAGCOT)[277] is a recently established partnership for developing commercial agriculture in Tanzania. The partnership operates in the southern corridor, a region roughly one-third the size of the country, which is rich in agricultural land. Tanzania's southern corridor links the port Daar es Salaam to Malawi, Zambia and the Democratic Republic of Congo, making it an important trade route. The partnership focuses on smallholder farmers and local communities, with the ultimate goal of pulling millions out of poverty.

In 2008 the UN General Assembly adopted the concept of developing Agriculture Growth Corridors in Africa. The Tanzanian plan for the Southern Growth Corridor was originated by the Tanzania National Business Council in 2009 through a policy initiative called Kilimo Kwanza.[278] Kilimo Kwanza calls for increasing private sector investment in agriculture that will promote the development of a modern and profitable agriculture sector in Tanzania. Developing the southern corridor has the potential to make East Africa entirely food-secure. Tanzania has the potential to become a major food exporter, rivaling Brazil.[279]

In May 2010, the Tanzanian president Jakaya Kikwete announced the launching of the SAGCOT at the WEF on Africa Summit. In his speech, Kikwete emphasized the need to transform the sector from "backward agriculture to modern agriculture". The president emphasized the need for leveraging the experience and resources of the private sector and the need for collaboration between farmers, agriculture companies and the government. The partnership will operate with a $50 million "Catalytic

Fund", for which USAID has already committed $2 million.[280] The first step in establishing the partnership was creating a working group to meet periodically and create a working plan. The working group developed documents that will guide the operations of the partnership.

The partnership formed an Executive Committee, composed of representatives of Unilever, Yara International, Agricultural Council of Tanzania, Alliance for a Green Revolution in Africa, Confederation of Tanzanian Industries, Tanzania Sugarcane Growers Association, USAID and the Irish Embassy in Tanzania. The Executive Committee was tasked with developing an investment blueprint for the corridor. Additional corridor partners include Diageo, DuPont, General Mills, Monsanto, SAB Miller, Syngenta, Standard Bank, National Microfinance Bank, NorFund, Food and Agriculture Organization (FAO), and the WEF.

The first publication of the partnership was the SAGCOT Concept Note, which was developed by the Agricultural Council of Tanzania with the assistance of AgDevCo and Prorustica.[281] The Concept Note describes the general plan for developing the corridor, which includes how to distribute financing and bring partners together. According to Patrick Guyver, Managing Director of ProRustica, the corridor approach was adopted for Tanzania after the implementation of a similar development program in Mozambique was successful in attracting commercial investment.[282]

The Concept Note defines SAGCOT's strategy as "breaking the impasse of agriculture development" by catalyzing large volumes of private investment and enabling regions with high potential for agriculture output to increase international competitiveness. The impasse mentioned in the strategy is caused by a combination of factors, including a non-friendly business environment that deters private investment and low demand for agriculture products that results in a disincentive for service companies to invest in infrastructure development in the region. The strategy for the corridor will be implemented in the following way:

1. Identifying areas with high agricultural potential and adequate access to existing infrastructure
2. Analysing the constraints on commercial agriculture and how they may be addressed
3. Establishing an organization focused on partnership-creation that ensures that programs in the private and public sectors are focused and coordinated
4. Provisioning support to the commercial agriculture sector through a new financing mechanism. Access to the mechanism will be

conditional based on the incorporation of smallholder farmers and local communities into the sector

5.   Recognizing the important roles played by the public and private sector actors to the successful execution of this approach.

The partnership is planning to facilitate the development of several clusters of profitable small, medium, and large-scale farms and associated agribusinesses throughout the corridor. Thus far, six clusters have been identified: Sumbawanga, Ihemi, Kilombero, Mbarali, Ludewa, and Rufiji.

The Concept Note identifies four requirements for the success of Kilimo Kwanza – finance, project development management, successful partnership, and favorable business and regulatory environments. Long-term, low-cost capital is needed to finance large infrastructure projects that will support the development of a successful and competitive agriculture sector in Tanzania. The management of project development will be conducted by a project development company that will be able to secure early-stage opportunities and work with them until they become attractive to private investors. The company will be responsible for:

- Securing long-term land agreements
- Conducting feasibility and technical studies
- Issuing soil analysis and trial planting
- Conducting consultations with local communities and government officials
- Developing business and financial plans
- Ensuring strong links to smallholder and emergent farmers
- Soliciting interest from commercial farmers and farming companies
- Securing off-take agreements
- Arranging financing and credit guarantees.

The success of Kilimo Kwanza also requires establishing a partnership organization, a neutral entity tasked with carrying out "partnership brokerage" and bringing together stakeholders from government, the private sector, and the international community. Representatives from ProRustica have emphasized the importance of such an organization in coordinating the partnership: as any coordinating body run exclusively by either the public or private sector would be likely to be viewed with suspicion by partners from other sectors, the establishment of a neutral arbiter should reassure both partner organizations and investors. In proposing such a model, ProRustica and other advising organizations hope to follow the success of earlier, similarly organized efforts (for example in Mozambique); they further hope to create a replicable model for cross sector agricultural development projects to be implemented in other African countries.[283]

The Agricultural Council of Tanzania took an early lead in coordinating SAGCOT's structure, and was aided by representatives from government ministries in writing the Concept Note. The last element described in the Concept Note as a necessity for the success of a commercial agriculture sector is improving the business and policy environments so that they support the development of the sector.

The Concept Note addresses three possible risks that SAGCOT faces and describes how they will be addressed. First, there is a risk that smallholder farmers and local communities will not benefit from commercial agriculture. The partnership addresses this risk by providing equitable financing to all farmers. The second risk identified is the environmental damage that will result from commercializing agriculture in Tanzania. The partnership will mitigate this risk by providing information on sustainable environmental practices and by including environmental conditions to funds granted. The third risk addressed in the report is that the environmental and regulatory environments will not support commercial farming. The partnership mitigates this risk by garnering support from high-level government officials for SAGCOT and support for commercial farming from local decision-makers.

The success of the southern corridor depends on the development of infrastructure that will support agriculture activity – feeder roads, water distribution systems, electricity reticulation, and cold-storage facilities. For this purpose, the partnership will assist agriculture businesses by providing several types of financing. The partnership will allocate public funds for large infrastructure projects. Agriculture-supporting infrastructure, such as irrigation systems, will be funded through "patient capital" – long-term, low-cost financing. Smallholder support programs with targeted agendas will be financed through grants provided by the partnership. Lastly, commercial lending will be available for on-farm investment costs and working capital.

Following the Concept Note, the partnership completed a more comprehensive analysis and work plan titled the Investment Footprint.[284] The report found that a $3.4 billion investment in the corridor will result in tripling Tanzania's agriculture output over 20 years, achieving food security in the region, creating 420,000 jobs, and lifting two million people out of poverty.[285] The plan also states that $2.1 billion of socially responsible investment can be derived from the private sector.[286] Converting over 300,000 hectares of land for commercial agriculture use will result in annual revenues of $1.2 billion by 2030.

Yara International, a global fertilizer company, was the first investor in the partnership, announcing in January 2011 a $20 million investment into a new fertilizer terminal at the Dar es Salaam port.[287] The next steps for the partnership are to begin evaluating the established clusters. To date, there has been no monitoring or evaluation of the project's impact; however, future monitoring and evaluating efforts will be carried out on three levels: individual private investment level (to determine the impact of single investments on agricultural development); the amalgamated impact of private investments on the entire corridor; and the social impact (for example, how many smallholders are benefitting) of investments in the corridor.

As of November 2011, the SAGCOT development company has been established and has begun the work of attracting partner organizations. Simultaneously, the government of Tanzania has established (but is currently reorganizing) a single government organization which is charged with coordinating with external partners – a promising development which, by creating a single contact point with the government for project partners, will eliminate bureaucratic hurdles as the project moves forward.

To date, SAGCOT organizers have met with a few major challenges. First of all, the financing center (Catalytic Fund) has been slower than expected in development and expansion – this is attributed to the need for transparency in its structure and operations before it can attract a large number of international investors. International recognition has been greater than expected. While this may be helpful in some ways, some believe that the high level of scrutiny may hinder real progress.

Nevertheless, SAGCOT partners remain optimistic and pleased with the project's progress thus far. Furthermore, they believe that the project's momentum – the engagement of the WEF and the international attention garnered by the effort – spells real promise for their hopes of replicating the model in other African nations.[288]

SAGCOT takes a different approach to poverty alleviation, emphasizing business development for farmers as a catalyst to address the various concerns facing these populations. This partnership strategy leverages investments and other resources to increase the capacity of smaller-scale farmers. As is the case in many initiatives designed to reduce poverty, there is no guarantee that the partnership's efforts will reach those most in need. But SAGCOT appears well positioned to become a compelling model for an economic development pathway to reduce poverty and strengthen subsistence in impoverished rural communities.

Poverty reduction is the greatest challenge facing the twenty-first century. While emerging partnerships are beginning to put critical pieces in place, the level of work to be done remains tremendous. The MDGs place an important visible emphasis on the persistence of poverty and its many effects. The MDGs have elevated the ambition to achieve concrete goals that can transform lives. Sustained momentum will be required to affect lives at a massive scale. Indeed, no goals will be achieved without ongoing collaboration.

The intended beneficiaries of poverty alleviation cannot merely receive services passively. Their engagement in the kinds of partnerships herein helps define the nature of problems, enhances the cultural relevance of strategies to address these problems, and provides ongoing checks and balances to strengthen impact.

PART IV

Challenges and opportunities going forward

13. The viability of partnerships

These numerous examples of cross sector partnerships in this book provide snapshots of different efforts to address important social and economic concerns by joining resources and transcending the public, private, and nonprofit sectors. These examples demonstrate what is possible within a range of structural and organizational frameworks. To varying degrees, these approaches have achieved results in how they have been launched and maintained over time. Some of these efforts have achieved measurable goals, while others have been more successful in designing structures that can continually produce results.

In the aggregate, these examples suggest that cross sector partnerships can be viable paths to address issues such as public health and employment. It is less clear what it would take to create a series of partnerships that could collectively make inroads around critical social concerns at a truly transformative scale. As noted, these collaborative formations are difficult to create and sustain. However, greater knowledge in recent years about what works effectively suggests that collaborative activity across sectors can increase their effectiveness across the board. This knowledge has the potential to inform existing partnerships and those yet to be initiated.

In order for widespread strategic cross sector partnerships to play a substantial role in changing the course of major societal concerns globally, much is required. First of all, a significant number of actors would have to be convinced of the viability of partnerships. Not everyone believes in the usefulness of cross sector collaboration in addressing such essential matters as literacy and hunger. And even in producing innovations that can lead to highly valuable technologies or industries, opinions vary around the role of the public sector in stimulating private enterprise. Secondly, even if the general public and various institutional leaders agree on the principles of cross sector collaboration, the capacity to develop and maintain a critical mass of effective partnerships simultaneously curing diseases and building roads may not exist. Philosophically, since many are not challenged to operate outside of their sectors or even their industries or singular institutions, some new change in mindset is necessary to enable new capacities. And, beyond changed thinking, partnerships call for atypical actions. They suggest a range of new competencies to navigate the various aforementioned barriers to effective partnerships.

At this moment, it is difficult to imagine most cross sector collaborations succeeding easily. However, because trial and error has led so many to conclude that today's complex challenges will only lessen dramatically when various resources are combined across sectors and focused on clear goals, partnerships will likely continue to proliferate. Indeed, this is a unique form of entrepreneurship. And, there may be some correlation between the relative success rates of partnerships and those of start-up businesses.

Ralph Smith said of the similar experiences between partnerships and emerging businesses, "Quite often partnerships, like any enterprise, are entered into with a surplus of good intentions. Everybody who starts a business thinks they're going to succeed; and like any strategy, you've got to say, first of all is this thing possible? Does it pass the laugh test?"[289] As in any enterprise, no one is certain of the long-term viability of a new idea. Like emerging businesses, partnerships must blend a combination of optimism and realism in assessing their prospects. Natalie Abatemarco suggested, "I've seen people stay in too long, because they can't walk away from that outcome. I've seen people give up too soon, and then see it happen anyway by somebody else …"[290]

Whichever the circumstance, partnerships require a healthy balance of hope and pessimism. Greater knowledge about what works, however, can increase participants' confidence about the potential viability of a given effort. Clarity about the resources and capabilities required to achieve goals can also increase viability. The enthusiasm that stimulates the creation of many partnerships must transcend ideas. Ira Harkavy warns of "messianic impotence". He indicated, "When you're just messianic, you go around saying, hey this is great stuff, and you don't get anything done. What do you need concretely on the ground to show you're making a success?"[291] To Harkavy, it is important to enter partnerships with practical and clear direction. He said, "So we never had at the beginning the sufficiency tests that we would really need, but we had a theory of change – whether it was right or wrong, whether it will be proven to be effective, we'll see …"[292]

Approaches to defining goals in early stages are shaped by the nature of the partnership and its intentions. The viability of a partnership depends on the magnitude of its goals. Efforts seeking a discrete change within a small timeframe are more likely to succeed in achieving their intended ends. But the relative capacity of partners involved, the resources at the table and the degree of collective will or urgency are also critical to viability. Partnerships with multiple partners and substantial long-term goals are challenged to manage their efforts in realistic increments. According to Ralph Smith:

> ... sustainability is going to depend upon a belief that you're making progress. So you need some of these confidence-building moments; and those confidence-building moments come with having achieved some milestones along the way ... Part of it I think is taking a deep breath and bring able to celebrate the half a loaf, or the half step and use that as fuel to go take the next.[293]

Assessment at the outset to diagnose a problem and strategically determine the most appropriate solution and the ingredients needed to create a collaborative effort is essential to viability. But this kind of reflective thinking is required throughout, as it enables partnerships to identify and acknowledge accomplishments as well as change course where necessary. The selection of problems, goals, processes, and structures inform partnerships' viability. Those efforts that attempt to address problems that outstrip their capacity are destined to fail. This is similarly true about goals, structures, and the programs developed to achieve goals. But problem identification is especially critical. First of all, cross sector partnerships are formed because resources and expertise from multiple spheres are required to address the matter at hand. Chong-Lim Lee said of problem identification, "I think there are probably still many problems that can be solved by technical siloed approaches. Where that works, that's wonderful."[294]

Indeed, partnerships are significant because they are required in particular, not all, circumstances. On the one hand, some matters do not require a great deal of cross sector collaboration. In fact, in instances where a single institution is best suited to address a problem, a partnership may do more harm than good. And, on the other hand, regarding those areas that truly require cross sector engagement, it is critical to stay within realistic bounds. The capacity of partnerships can be assessed on many levels.

One significant characteristic of the nature of complexity in our contemporary world is the altered role or influence of nation-states. The "war on terror" has been an attempt to halt the activities of a global network. The concept of cross sector collaboration rests within this context. Sovereign nations are determining how to address, what Ralph Smith calls, "asymmetrical threats".[295] The global economy and the war on terror both represent extreme degrees of integrated impact: the entire globe is affected by actions in these arenas. Acts of terror have redefined the daily existence of people across the globe, and economic volatility in a single environment can send shockwaves throughout global markets. This kind of integrated experience suggests integrated action.

A great challenge to the viability of many cross sector partnerships is the intersection of many issues. Matters such as health, hunger, and poverty do not exist in isolation. So, while partnerships attempt to focus, they must also recognize a broader context. Ultimate solutions will not only require multiple participants across sectors, but approaches that respect and recognize multi-issue contexts.

Partnerships have the potential to complement public services, even keep vital programs afloat. A central reason for the proliferation of partnerships has been the continued constraints on governments. The need for services does not disappear in the absence of adequate public financing. Governments are continually forced to cut services when confronted by difficult choices to balance budgets. Public officials are increasingly looking to private resources to offset some of the limitations created by cutbacks. This is unlikely a permanent solution, but a viable approach to sustaining public initiatives. Denice Williams, an agency executive for the City of New York, works in an area of government that often faces budgetary reductions – youth services. She reflected, "... the non-mandated services are the first services to be cut – the youth development, the afterschool, the summer youth employment ... public private partnerships has been a key strategy for our department to try to maintain and many times grow services available to young people."[296]

Collaboration with government is critical to the viability of any cross sector partnership. With goals to improve economies, health care, hunger, and others, partnerships can only remain viable over time with support from government. Governments are consistently required to provide social services and establish policies that enhance the public good. A partnership with private entities to improve education, for example, might impact a few over a certain period. With the participation of government, these efforts are poised to influence service delivery impacting the entire population of a given municipality or nation. It is government's responsibility to maintain the infrastructure and services benefitting the public. Public private partnerships do not replace government's role. Ideally, they complement public policy and services harmoniously.

Strategic partnerships are aware of these dynamics, and recognize that longer-term impact is more likely when the represented sectors mutually respect and recognize their respective roles. However, many complications can stand in the way of progress. Viable cross sector partnerships tend to benefit from preconditions. For example, corrupt or inefficient governments create barriers for strategic partnerships. Private or nongovernmental participants might not trust governments, or see their role as demonstrating to governments how programs should be implemented. All contexts contain circumstances that shape how partnerships form, succeed, or fail.

According to Louis Elneus, too many private and nongovernmental partners are working independently in Haiti, and not cooperating with the Haitian government. He said, "… part of the problem prior to the earthquake still continues, because organizations are doing things by themselves. And the results – we still have 1.5 million in tents. And you see how organizations are just refusing to work with local government …"[297] Responding to a disaster inherently requires coordination among many actors across sectors and industries. Disasters bring sweeping impact, touching all facets of life with a palpable sense of urgency. This immediate need for a response can stimulate action across the board. Individuals and institutions want to get involved in some way, but not always in coordination.

Partnerships with highly focused particular goals rest within a different set of dynamics. Pfizer serves its specific mission when it focuses on a particular disease or other health condition. The company has a vested interest in increasing use of its products and securing cooperation from governments, civil society, and other relevant private entities. As Rekha Chalasani suggests, "that portion of the population globally, who may not be able to afford our medicines or have access to our medicines through an effective public health care infrastructure, is absolutely part of our overall mission."[298] Here again, recognition of interests and roles can help frame partnerships' intentions. Pfizer acknowledges its interests, but remains continually cognizant of the health care infrastructure in the nations in which medicines can be distributed. The function of local government to receive and administer Pfizer's medications is vital. The overall public and private health infrastructure in any given nation is essential to distributing medicine.

In the Haitian context according to Elneus, the local health care infrastructure is not benefitting from the involvement of outsiders. He said, "For example, Doctors Without Borders – they're providing all their medical assistance for free. But it's not working, right? Because it is closing clinics, private clinics, and creating a greater need."[299] Local context is essential. The more that partnerships adequately assess local contexts before proceeding, the more likely they will succeed. Viable partnerships work in harmony with existing contexts. They are able to predict the repercussions of their actions based on awareness of existing dynamics.

Elneus' insights are informed by experience in Haiti, and in leading a small nongovernmental organization. According to Elneus, many small community-based organizations are left out of various cross sector partnerships. Small organizations must be strategic in finding influential partners through which they can gain access. In reference to the Bill and Melinda Gates Foundation, Elneus said, "Often Gates will not give money to a local community in need. But they will give money to a program at Columbia University."[300] Chalasani concurred, but provided additional insight on the constraints facing a major corporation like Pfizer in directly interfacing with local entities around the world. She said, "The US Government has a regulation called the Foreign Corrupt Practices Act. So that's something that Pfizer actively, in all of its endeavors, needs to comply with. So right now, it's extraordinarily difficult for us to provide grants to local indigenous organizations."[301]

The viability of partnerships is also dependent upon the actions of the individuals within them. Leadership can make the difference in partnerships' relative success. Since these collaborative efforts are new formations transcending organizational boundaries, they require different viewpoints and approaches. Their many parts call for an extraordinary style of management. John Heller of Synergos stresses "bridging leadership" in partnerships – "that leadership paradigm that naturally looks across and beyond borders, to look at the system, to look at the synergies, to bring the key people together to say, 'time out, what's going on within this whole system?'"[302]

In some ways, this understanding of complex multi-stakeholder arrangements belies the specialist training all professionals receive. Thus, when considering the viability of partnerships over time, it is clear that training tailored specifically to managing for collaboration would be necessary. Partnerships require a different mindset and particular skills based on spanning boundaries rather than working within them.

Overall, partnerships can become viable means to meeting critical social and economic ends. However, they face substantial complications between sectors and within political and cultural contexts. Better understanding of the uniqueness of these formations should enhance their long-term viability.

14. Steps forward

While cross sector partnerships have proliferated and matured, it is clear that much work is required to enhance their practice and ultimate effectiveness. Outside, informed perspectives can intervene to strengthen partnerships. As with singular organizations, informed outsiders can independently diagnose partnerships' challenges and opportunities. At every stage, partnerships can benefit from guidance from a third party. Moreover, it is critical to recognize the numerous categories partnerships must consider for their ongoing capacity.

MARGA INCORPORATED

Marga Incorporated, the company founded by the author in 2000, provides strategic advice and research to philanthropic initiatives and partnerships. Marga developed a methodology to advise and strengthen partnerships based on observations of partnership tendencies and direct experience in consulting actual cross sector collaborations. It addresses partnerships' needs in nine categories:

- Assessment
- Identifying partners
- Establishing win/win possibilities
- Convening partners
- Conducting relevant research
- Facilitating strategic plans
- Designing projects
- Creating products
- Evaluating progress.

Assessment

As previously noted, preconditions prior to partnerships' creation can shape the approach to developing a collaborative effort. Thorough assessment can surface political, cultural, and capacity considerations vital to a partnership's long-term potential. Assessment is a critical component of the upfront work emphasized by participants in partnerships. Entering blindly can be highly detrimental. Awareness of essential dynamics allows partnerships to incorporate potential pitfalls into their plans. Effective assessment can make the difference in helping partnerships evolve strategically, making logical decisions and establishing realistic goals. Assessment sheds light on potential limitations and helps partnerships stay within themselves. As noted repeatedly by focus group participants, not every issue requires the combined effort of representatives of the public, private, and social sectors. Assessment can help partnerships identify the most appropriate issues to address.

Identifying Partners

Who is at the table can define the quality and potential of a partnership. Participants should match goals and intentions. Many collaborative efforts begin with those who are willing to be involved. While self-selection can go a long way in maintaining enthusiasm and interest, it may not cover all of the skills and experiences required for the partnership's success. Furthermore, at every stage, the composition of participants is relevant. The mix of partners best suited in the beginning may not be appropriate in later stages. At the outset, partnerships require vision and commitment, and an ability to transition from theory to practice. Over time, more specific expertise might be required as implementation becomes the primary focus. Partnerships' capacity to meet their goals is dependent upon their participants. Overall, all collaborative initiatives should continually consider the composition of their partners, clarify the skills and experiences required to fulfil stated goals, and recruit when necessary to fill gaps.

Establishing Win/Win Possibilities

Mutual benefit among participants can be critical to forming and sustaining partnerships. All partners involved stand to gain in some way from mutual pursuits, but all partners do not always collectively understand or recognize their respective interests. Focus group participants continually referenced the importance of trust and communication. A critical component of this is transparency across the board about vested interests. As early as possible, partnerships should surface the respective vested interests of participants, and seek to forge mutual benefit out of these varied priorities. Not only will this deliberate action create symbiosis among participants, it will enhance the long-term sustainability of the effort. As many partnerships must continue to revive their purpose and actively keep their participants interested, those involved are more likely to stick around when they understand how they are benefitting.

Convening Partners

The process of bringing partners together to engage in productive communication also requires attention. Perceptions of who leads a partnership can create tension. Scenarios vary, but a partnership ideally establishes a degree of equality among participants. When one single partner is responsible for convening all of the other partners, some may be suspicious. A third party can play the role of, what Marga calls, a "partnership catalyst" – an entity solely responsible for assisting a partnership's launching and maintenance. This role is somewhat of a managing agent that is not one of the partners, but the convener. This action avoids placing a single partner in the awkward position of convening the others while attempting to remain equal to the other representatives. The convening role is also an independent mediating capacity that can more honestly navigate dialogue. As many of the focus group participants indicated, an honest broker facilitates more authentic communication among partners. As demonstrated in the case examples, partnerships structure this convening and brokering arrangement in various capacities, some through actual new organizations responsible for managing partnerships, and others with third party coordinators.

Conducting Relevant Research

The growth and development of partnerships over recent years provides valuable knowledge that can inform the future quality of collaboration. Many partnerships in formation feel uncertain about how to structure their efforts and establish appropriate goals and programs. An under-standing of how existing seasoned partnerships have developed and progressed can provide informed guidance to emerging efforts. Research on promising practices and potential pitfalls can be instructive to partnerships. Ideally, over time the quality of the development and implementation of these efforts will continue to increase as they learn lessons from the past. Since these collaborations could very well become new models of governance upon which populations rely to resolve pressing concerns, research to improve practice is highly significant. Partnerships can benefit both from a general understanding of what works in cross sector collaboration and also specific case examples. Additionally, a third party can provide customized research on the local context in which a given partnership is situated, and the capacity and interests of prospective partners.

Facilitating Strategic Plans

Strategic planning can help partnerships clarify direction and establish realistic goals and programs. In these volatile times, all entities are challenged to control their future over the long term. But planning is still relevant in comprehensively reflecting upon potential barriers and opportunities, and accurately diagnosing problems to be addressed. Strategic planning encourages partnerships to craft a broad vision for the future, perhaps three to five years forward. This vision could include an overview of programmatic and structural components, providing a clearer sense of why the partnership exists. As partnerships sometimes lose a sense of direction, an established vision statement can remind them that their purpose transcends going through the motions. From a long-range vision, partnerships can construct specific programming, adequate staffing and infrastructure, realistic financing, and models for revenue generation in the shorter term.

Designing Projects

Transitioning from a longer range vision and a strategic plan to implementation can be difficult for many partnerships. The passion and sense of purpose that brings various partners to the table initially is not always followed by practical and effective implementation. Moreover, bigger issues and concerns tend to galvanize participants to work together across sector boundaries, but partnerships can only meet their goals with more mundane, granular practices day to day. Because wider ideas stimulate initial enthusiasm, it is important to guide partnerships toward greater specificity. Typically, a partnership is more likely to progress toward its vision with an inaugural project – a particular program that characterizes the partnership's intentions that is likely to achieve visible and measurable results in the short term. This kind of signature project can potentially pivot emerging partnerships from a building and visioning stage toward implementation. This is one of the more critical challenges to partnerships' evolution. Many collaborative initiatives can remain somewhat stuck for years in initial meeting and planning. While upfront investment in communication and relationship building is essential, as the focus group participants underscored, it is important to recognize when and how to shift toward implementation. Specific signature projects can assist this progression. They should not replace continuous dialogue, but they can bolster the significance of partnership by producing results. Measurable results from these projects can demonstrate the partnership's value, which can encourage participants to continue to move forward.

Creating Products

The results of signature projects can be essential to strengthening continuity and staying on mission. However small, measurable impact demonstrates progress. Participants need to be reminded that their involvement is a valuable use of time. They have many competing priorities, especially given that the partnership is not their primary responsibility. Keeping partners involved is a continuous concern in any collaboration with long-term intentions. Acknowledging, capturing, and celebrating progress is important to deepening commitment among participants. Moreover, developing products can not only encourage participants, but wider audiences with an interest in the partnership's work. Progress reports, publications, and other materials capturing progress can build goodwill overall, not to mention increase visibility and revenue. Depending on the partnership's goals, communications materials and other products can widen support. While all partnerships maintain a core group of participants, they also have outer circles of interested parties. Products significantly facilitate communication with these wider networks.

Evaluating Progress

Evaluation is a necessity for any organization or multi-stakeholder formation. Given partnerships' multifaceted complexity, it is even more critical to build in evaluation mechanisms. Signature projects can refine specificity out of long-range visions for the future. Success is measured on many levels. From more general goals, partnerships can identify specific indicators of progress on all aspects from programs to the process of working collaboratively. The participation of multiple stakeholders and the many features comprising collaborative initiatives suggest multidimensional metrics. The process of how partnerships evolve is highly significant. Much of the work of these efforts is to convene disparate representatives of sectors unaccustomed to collaborating. This endeavor requires tasks worthy of measurement. In many instances, merely bringing and keeping partners at the table is an achievement in itself. However, this is not enough. Evaluated progress around process should always balance alongside programmatic impact and results. A partnership seeking to reduce the spread of a disease cannot fully gain value by joining relevant actors together. At some point, this partnership must demonstrate actual numerical progress against the disease. Moreover, both quantitative and qualitative evaluation methods can demonstrate relative success. Sometimes stories capturing multiple aspects of the partnership's work can showcase various nuances that would not surface in numbers alone.

All nine of these categories demonstrate how partnerships can increase their effectiveness. Additionally, they illuminate the wide range of considerations required to navigate many moving parts. Indeed, all singular organizations must address the same range of issues, which are multiplied by the complexity of partnerships.

Recently, Marga Incorporated applied this methodology in advising the Port Richmond Partnership[303] of Staten Island. Led by Wagner College, a private institution of higher education in the New York City Borough of Staten Island, this partnership connects a wide range of local NGOs, public officials, hospitals, and corporations. As it approached its third year of existence, this partnership desired a strategic planning process to clarify its long-range direction. Wagner College, under the leadership of President Richard Guarasci, secured funding from a local foundation to cover the cost of the process.

Marga interviewed numerous stakeholders in the region to gain a better sense of the appropriate programming and structure for the partnership. The partnership addresses health, education, economic development, and immigration in its programming. Stakeholders largely affirmed this content. The partnership's structure was still in formation. Stakeholder feedback helped clarify the appropriate model for governance and ongoing communication with stakeholders. As a result of this process, the Port Richmond Partnership clarified its long-range programmatic and structural goals. It also refined the partnership's projects, as it enters an intermediate phase of development.

Partnership Life Cycles

Additionally, any attempts to strengthen partnerships should take account of life cycles. Just as all formations evolve over time, partnerships' priorities shift based on their stages of development. These efforts progress along a continuum, and should be understood accordingly. In evaluating progress, it is difficult to expect dramatic measurable impact in the early stages. Because substantial effort is needed merely to establish the group and agree upon goals, creating a functional partnership with clear intentions is significant progress. Context along a continuum helps establish realistic expectations.

Priorities are different in the *initial phase* of partnerships' development, than in the *long term* or the *intermediate phase.* In order to assess progress within the context of a partnership's life cycle, it is important to clarify goals and phases of development accordingly. All partnerships have long-term goals with concrete anticipated quantitative results. However, because so many actors are involved representing different sectors and cultures, the quality of engagement among partners is critical to measure as well.

One way to conceptualize a framework for evaluating a partnership's progress is to simultaneously include measuring progress (taking into account phases of development as well as a combination of long-term quantitative metrics), along with quantitative results that emphasize the nature of collaboration (how effectively are partners working with each other?).

Table 14.1   Framework for evaluating a partnership's progress

Initial Phase	Intermediate Phase	Long Term	Continuous
Acquiring and applying knowledge	Identifying signature projects and goals	Achieving measurable long-term quantitative goals	Monitoring the quality of engagement and inclusion of partners
Mobilizing relevant stakeholders	Implementing plans and projects	Developing products capturing results	Assessing progress toward intended goals
Establishing long-range plans and anticipated results	Revising long-term goals where necessary	Refining the quality of implementation	Making mid-course corrections where necessary
Creating an appropriate structure for the partnership	Clarifying mutual benefit to involved partners		Reporting progress to stakeholders

This framework is not intended to address every single consideration a partnership might confront, but it distinguishes priorities based on phases of development. Moreover, it highlights the continuous attention partnership participants and leaders must pay to the quality of a given partnership's processes. Partnerships' effectiveness is shaped by their attention to both longer-term measurable results and processes throughout a life cycle of development. Indeed, some partnerships are intentionally short term, and collaborations do not tend to unfold linearly. However, all partnerships undergo initial phases to establish plans and goals, execute those plans in an intermediate phase, and hope to achieve intended results with an ability to demonstrate those accomplishments. Moreover, all partnerships require attention to process dynamics that include the quality of engagement among participating stakeholders.

Strategic planning, reflection, and assessment are not one-time events. These managerial tools are not only continuous for all singular organizations; their significance is magnified in multi-stakeholder partnerships. Because of their complicated structures, the management of partnerships requires exceptional attention. Not all partnerships maintain the capacity and resources to provide this level of management. Most of the cases discussed in this book have built this degree of capacity; however, all partnerships are challenged to sustain the requisite resources over time. Cross sector partnerships comprise representatives of other organizations. Partnership participants are primarily concerned with the organizations they represent. Partnerships are challenged to create new governance structures that are solely focused on managing collaborative entities themselves.

Resources to support these structures often come from partners themselves. However, in the face of restricted government budgets and a general economic slowdown, partnerships will rely on creativity to maintain their efforts. The more partners benefit from their involvement in collaborative initiatives, the more likely partnerships can sustain their efforts. When representatives are realizing mutual benefit, involvement in partnerships becomes an investment. Time and resources devoted to partnerships are more justifiable when all partnerships can make a solid case for their continued involvement.

15. Conclusions and recommendations

Governance and problem-solving into the future will require creativity. The boundaries in which resources and expertise are situated must be crossed. In order to transcend sector boundaries and harness the assets that can be applied to our most pressing concerns, policy makers and leaders of various forms must pursue collaboration. New collaborative formations that combine the strengths of representatives across sectors bring their own priorities and needs. Forging cross sector partnerships is one tremendous step in itself. But if these efforts are to become viable and reliable sources of development and innovation, it is critical to enhance their effectiveness.

As these partnerships proliferate, their success varies. A number of case examples have been able to begin achieving their intended results, but much is to be learned about how to routinely create and maintain effective and strategic partnerships. If increasingly complex contexts will require cross sector collaboration, it is imperative to understand the ingredients of effective partnerships. Various considerations can contribute to understanding what it will take to understand and improve partnerships.

Strategic partnerships must be applicable to *urban and rural contexts*. First of all, urbanization is changing the global landscape. As populations increasingly shift to cities, urban strategies become even more significant. The general needs of populations are becoming urban needs. The context of cities brings unique circumstances to take into account. Additionally, mega cities also deserve particular attention, as they contain magnified challenges and complex systems with numerous influential institutions. These cities also wield substantial global influence, affecting the wellbeing of entire nations and continents.

Rural contexts are losing populations, but not relevance. The natural resources that serve an increasingly urbanized world still remain in rural areas. Agriculture and mining are still significant. Rural populations exist in wider spaces that are disconnected: populations are closely knit, but within relatively isolated contexts. The challenge in urban contexts is to forge coordination among entities in close proximity. In rural environments, the challenge is to connect isolated communities to the nearest region. The great issues reflected in the MDGs are all manifested in both urban and rural areas. The matters of education, the environment, hunger, and health are all manifested locally. Strategic partnerships can bring relevant representatives together across sectors to jointly address these issues. However they cannot adequately take on these challenges without working within particular local conditions and nuances.

Similarly, it is important to consider *developed and emerging* national contexts in shaping collaborative arrangements. Strategic partnerships take into account national conditions. Some emerging countries might experience rapid economic growth and substantial population transitions from urban to rural environments. However, they may contain undeveloped social services and public infrastructure. Some developed countries might experience economic decline and shrinking government budgets. However, they many include well-developed infrastructure and enduring institutions. Partnership strategies in some developed environments might emphasize building from longstanding local assets, while those in emerging environments might emphasize building anew.

Rural and urban as well as developed and emerging environments must address *concentrated poverty*. Urbanization helps raise the standard of living generally, but population increases have also proven to increase the presence of crowded low-income neighborhoods. In emerging nations, this concentration is more palpable, but even in well-developed cities like New York, the poverty that exists is concentrated in particular areas. Moreover, even in rural environments, lower-income populations live among themselves. This geographical reality isolates impoverished communities from resources. Partnerships have the potential to make unprecedented connections, and link low-income residents to public and private resources. The social sector is poised to increase the likelihood that lower-income populations are participating in strategic partnerships. Since the types of concerns in the MDGs cannot be addressed without improving the lives of low-income communities, strategic partnerships must be inclusive.

As partnerships transcend boundaries, their inclusion must overcome *inequalities based on difference*. Demographic changes in the many developed nations, for example, demonstrate increased immigrant populations and inequality based on race and ethnicity. Gender inequality remains persistent across the globe. Truly developed societies cannot afford substantial inequality. They have a vested interest in an educated and skilled population, which can produce and innovate over time. Strategic partnerships must adequately address racial and gender inequality in order to address the great challenges facing cities, towns, and nations.

A global economy based on knowledge and technology is driven by *innovation and business development*. In some contexts, industrial clusters have built business and job opportunities by galvanizing public and private partners around growing a specific industry. This single industry approach is one way in which collaboration can stimulate innovation and business development. Other strategies will be required to incubate new businesses, encourage entrepreneurs, and invest in relevant research. This level of coordination should include higher education, enterprising individuals, private industry, and others. These strategies can stimulate economic opportunities. The extent of these opportunities (e.g. the degree to which they extend to low-income communities) requires deliberate attention.

Ensuring benefits to low-income communities from economic development can be facilitated by the social sector. The involvement of the nonprofit sector in public private partnerships has the potential to round out the entire picture. *Appreciation for the nonprofit sector* can widen the benefits of partnerships and increase their impact on some of today's most pressing issues. The social sector represents civil society; and the organizations in this sector often work directly on behalf of populations typically disconnected from influential collaborative initiatives. Additionally, many other formations, such as neighborhood associations, which are not necessarily formally incorporated, are other important avenues toward broader participation. Furthermore, the range of types of NGOs includes some important influential entities, such as universities.

Universities, hospitals, and some other enduring organizations represent *anchor institutions*. These entities are unlikely to leave their locations, thus they are rooted in their surrounding communities. This level of stability makes anchor institutions important reliable resources to local economies. Often the most substantial nongovernmental local employers in their regions, these anchor institutions can play unique roles in strategic partnerships. Because they are grounded in their settings, they are poised to remain committed within longstanding partnerships to address concerns that transcend generations, such as schools, health, the environment, and the economy. Additionally, they house diverse resources – knowledge, jobs, human capital, land and facilities, and so on. Local governments are increasingly looking toward their anchor institutions to help address a variety of issues. While some areas across the globe might not contain vast well-resourced anchor institutions, they likely contain some form of enduring institutions. Strategic partnerships build from their local assets to forge approaches to improve the future.

Another important dimension of the social sector's contribution to partnerships is *philanthropy*. Inherently cross sector collaborations, grant-making foundations leverage private resources to address various socio-economic concerns. Beyond their resources, foundations are positioned to convene various parties across sectors. Locally focused foundations are uniquely situated to coordinate within specific geographical settings. Many partnerships are challenged to finance their activities over the long term. Often more flexible than financing from other sectors, foundation resources can help partnerships innovate and sustain their efforts.

While partnerships might enhance how various concerns are addressed, they do not automatically and organically emerge. Perhaps in crisis situations, various parties feel the urgency to join together, but typically, those who create partnerships are highly dedicated. The success of partnerships will depend upon *commitment across sectors* to transcend boundaries for collaboration. When leadership across different institutions in all three sectors view working jointly across sectors as a priority, partnerships will expand and improve. Indeed, a corporation might serve a vested interest by participating in a cross sector partnership. But, when the greater goals of the partnership are of central interest to this corporation, the collaborative effort in itself is in a stronger position. In order for partnerships to become viable and effective, their participants should increase their level of dedication to collaborative efforts. It is unrealistic for governments and institutions to treat partnerships on a par with organizational or agency priorities, but partnerships can become extensions of those priorities.

While commitment at the leadership level remains a significant feature in partnerships, actually practicing partnerships is just as elusive. Effective practice in partnerships requires *a distinct mindset and unique competencies*. Decisions ordinarily made quickly with a few conversations may require many levels of dialogue to reach a conclusion in partnerships. A different degree of patience is essential in effective collaborative efforts. The ability to work with difference, understand varying viewpoints or styles of work, and navigate group decision-making are among competencies that enable partnerships' success. Focus group participants highlighted a wide range of characteristics of partnerships that stakeholders in partnerships must prepare to face. Additional time to build relationships, establish trust, and construct healthy lines of communication make partnerships exceptional forms of governance and management. Participants in partnerships should be prepared to listen, respect other cultures, and strive for mutual benefit at magnified levels.

Partnerships can only evolve into reliable means of routinely addressing critical social problems and stimulating innovation with deliberate *strategies to enhance their effectiveness*. These complex efforts are proliferating, as leaders across sectors are concluding that new pathways can leverage resources across sectors to solve problems. But, partnerships' intricacies increase the margin for error. With many moving parts, partnerships require attention at every phase of development. Myriad challenges confront how partnerships form, advance, and succeed. The involvement of honest brokers can assist partnerships in handling the various unique nuances that can make the difference in success. Strategic partnerships can assess their contexts, select appropriate issues to address, and create realistic programs and structures. Enhancing all partnerships' ability to become more strategic will increase the potential of cross sector collaboration to routinely address critical global concerns.

The *scale* of these global concerns suggests not only an increase in collaborative activity, but substantially improved quality in the formation and implementation of partnerships. It is not too difficult to find specific case examples of cross sector partnerships around the world. It is more challenging to find partnerships that have successfully achieved their intended ends. But the level of cooperation and coordination that would be required to, for example, expedite visible progress toward the MDGs, is many times the collaborative activity under way. The level of required resources alone is challenging to mobilize. The process of joint action alongside funding exacerbates the enormity of the challenge. Nevertheless, before imagining a more macro-level new way of operating in all sectors, each existing partnership has the potential to increase its capacity and impact.

Each effective partnership is a story to pass on to other existing and prospective partnerships. *Research on and knowledge of* effective partnerships can raise standards and clarify what it takes to create and maintain collaborative efforts that successfully convene representatives across sectors, jointly establish goals, plan strategically, develop realistic programs, and achieve measurable progress. Two levels of research and knowledge development can increase understanding of the effectiveness of partnerships. The first level emphasizes broader characteristics and promising practices. Engagement with participants who have experienced numerous partnerships helps capture a picture of the promise and pitfalls of cross sector collaboration. This line of research includes continuous literature review, as the expanding base of scholarship on partnership rises with the proliferation of partnerships themselves. The second level of research is the continuous search for case examples of cross sector partnerships around the world, addressing varying issues and operating within different contexts. There is no singular version of a partnership that is equally instructive to all other collaborative initiatives. It is important to understand the range of manifestations of partnerships and simultaneously recognize the significance of contextual circumstances in shaping how collaboration emerges. Case examples are specific and even inspirational. The more variety among these efforts, the more others can find a bit of themselves in these stories.

As contexts change in our volatile world, partnerships will adapt accordingly. Consequently, research on partnerships is continually necessary. It is important to continually monitor partnerships around the world and engage practitioners on general questions of the value, limits, and potential of cross sector collaboration. Future research should also deepen investigation of select topics addressed by partnerships and particular case examples within those topics. Further investigation into particular examples illuminates the most specific nuances that shape the nature of collaborative initiatives.

Strategic partnerships stand to confront the most challenging issues of our times. These contemporary forms of governance and decision-making have the potential to make far greater strides into the future. Greater knowledge of what is required to improve partnerships and deliberate efforts to strengthen them can enhance the impact of these efforts. The magnitude of today's great challenges calls for new ways to harness resources from numerous entities and apply them to solve problems and innovate. An investment in stronger, more strategic, cross sector partnerships is an investment in a better world.

Notes

1. "We Can End Poverty 2015 Millennium Development Goals – Goal 1 Eradicate Extreme Poverty and Hunger Fact Sheet." UN website, accessed July 13, 2012 at http://www.un.org/millenniumgoals/pdf/MDG_FS_1_EN.pdf.
2. "The Millennium Development Goals Report." United Nations, 2011, p. 17.
3. "We Can End Poverty 2015 Millennium Development Goals – Goal 2 Achieve Universal Primary Education Fact Sheet." UN website, accessed July 13, 2012 at http://www.un.org/millenniumgoals/pdf/MDG_FS_2_EN.pdf.
4. "The Millennium Development Goals Report." United Nations, 2011, pp. 20–21.
5. "We Can End Poverty 2015 Millennium Development Goals – Goal 3 Promote Gender Equality and Empower Women Fact Sheet." UN website, accessed July 13, 2012 at http://www.un.org/millenniumgoals/pdf/MDG_FS_3_EN.pdf.
6. "The Millennium Development Goals Report." United Nations, 2011, p. 24.
7. Ibid, p. 27.
8. "We Can End Poverty 2015 Millennium Development Goals – Goal 4 Reduce Child Mortality Fact Sheet." UN website, accessed July 13, 2012 at http://www.un.org/millenniumgoals/pdf/MDG_FS_4_EN.pdf.
9. "The Millennium Development Goals Report." United Nations, 2011, p. 29.
10. "We Can End Poverty 2015 Millennium Development Goals – Goal 5 Improve Maternal Health Fact Sheet." UN website, accessed July 13, 2012 at http://www.un.org/millenniumgoals/pdf/MDG_FS_5_EN.pdf.
11. "The Millennium Development Goals Report." United Nations, 2011, p. 37.
12. "We Can End Poverty 2015 Millennium Development Goals – Goal 6 Combat AIDS/HIV, Malaria and Other Diseases Fact Sheet." UN website, accessed July 13, 2012 at http://www.un.org/millenniumgoals/pdf/MDG_FS_6_EN.pdf.
13. "The Millennium Development Goals Report." United Nations, 2011, p. 49.
14. "We Can End Poverty 2015 Millennium Development Goals – Goal 7 Ensure Environmental Sustainability Fact Sheet." UN website, accessed July 13, 2012 at http://www.un.org/millenniumgoals/pdf/MDG_FS_7_EN.pdf.
15. The MDGs promote the idea that the least developed countries are receiving assistance from other developing countries in the global south, which have greater resources; accessed July 13, 2012 at http://www.un.org/millenniumgoals/pdf/MDG_FS_8_EN.pdf.
16. "We Can End Poverty 2015 Millennium Development Goals – Goal 8 Develop a Global Partnership for Development Fact Sheet." UN website, accessed July 13, 2012 at http://www.un.org/millenniumgoals/pdf/MDG_FS_8_EN.pdf.
17. "The Millennium Development Goals Report." United Nations, 2011, p. 5.
18. "About Us." Clinton Global Initiative website, accessed July 13, 2012 at http://www.clintonglobalinitiative.org/aboutus/default.asp?Section=AboutUs&PageTitle=About%20Us.
19. "Members." World Economic Forum website, accessed July 13, 2012 at http://www.weforum.org/members.
20. Asian Development Bank (2008), *Public–Private Partnership Handbook*, p. 3, http://www.adb.org/sites/default/files/pub/2008/Public-Private-Partnership.pdf.

21. OECD.StatExtracts, *Central Government Debt*, accessed July 10, 2012 at http://stats.oecd.org/Index.aspx?datasetcode=GOV_DEBT#.
22. UN DESA (2009) *World Population Ageing 2009*, p. viii.
23. UNFPA (2007) *State of World Population 2007 – Unleashing the Potential of Urban Growth*, p. 1.
24. James E Austin. (2000), *The Collaboration Challenge: How Nonprofits and Businesses Succeed Through Strategic Alliances*, The Peter F. Drucker Foundation for Nonprofit Management.
25. Pauline Vaillancourt Rosenau, ed. (2000), *Public-Private Policy Partnerships*.
26. David Maurrasse, (2001), *Beyond the Campus: How Colleges and Universities Form Partnerships with their Communities*.
27. Michael Geddes (2005), *Making Public Private Partnerships Work: Building Relationships and Understanding Cultures*.
28. Graeme Hodge and Carsten Greve, eds. (2005) *The Challenge of Public Private Partnerships: Learning from International Experience*.
29. Pieter Glasbergen, Frank Biermann, and Arthur P.J. Mol. (2007) *Partnerships, Governance and Sustainable Development*.
30. National Research Council (2009), *Enhancing the Effectiveness of Sustainability Partnerships*.
31. Oliver W. Porter (2008), *Public/Private Partnerships for Local Government*.
32. Albert N. Link. (2006), *Public/Private Partnerships: Innovation Strategies and Policy Alternatives*.
33. Klaus Grebmer, Frank Hartwich, David J. Spielman (2010), "Public-Private Partnerships and Developing-Country Agriculture: Evidence from the International Agriculture Research System". *Public Administration and Development* 30, pp. 261–76.
34. Christian M. Rogerson (2010), "In Search of Public–Private Sector Partnerships for Local Economic Development in South Africa", *Urban Forum* 21, pp. 441–56.
35. Oana Branzei and Marlene J. Le Ber (2010), "Towards a Critical Theory of Value Creation in Cross-Sector Partnerships", *Organization* 17, p. 599.
36. Marlene J. Le Ber and Oana Branzei (2010), "(Re)Forming Strategic Cross-Sector Partnerships: Relational Processes of Social Innovation", *Business & Society* 49:1, March, pp. 140–72.
37. Rhys Andrews and Tom Entwistle (2010), "Does Cross-Sectoral Partnership Deliver? An Empirical Exploration of Public Service Effectiveness, Efficiency, and Equity", *Journal of Public Administration Research and Theory* 20, January, pp. 679–701.
38. Bradley K. Googins and Steven A. Rochlin (2000), "Creating the Partnership Society: Understanding the Rhetoric and Reality of Cross-Sectoral Partnerships", *Business and Society Review* 105:1, Spring, p. 127–44.
39. Dennis A. Rondinelli and Ted London (2003), "How corporations and environmental groups cooperate: Assessing cross-sector alliances and collaborations", *Academy of Management Executive* 17, pp. 61–76.
40. John M. Bryson, Barbara C. Crosby and Melissa Middleton Stone (2006), "The Design and Implementation of Cross-Sector Collaborations: Propositions from the Literature", *Public Administration Review* 66, December, pp. 44–55.
41. John W. Selsky and Barbara Parker (2005), "Cross-Sector Partnerships to Address Social Issues: Challenges to Theory and Practice", *Journal of Management* 31:6, December, pp. 849–73.
42. David Maurrasse (2001), *Beyond the Campus: How Colleges and Universities form Partnerships with Their Communities*.
43. Ralph Smith. Focus Group, November 15, 2010.
44. Swati Adarkar. Focus Group, November 15, 2010.
45. Natalie Abatemarco. Focus Group, November 15, 2010.
46. Natalie Abatemarco. Focus Group, November 15, 2010.

47. K.C. Burton. Focus Group, November 15, 2010.
48. Chong Lim-Lee. Focus Group, November 15, 2010.
49. Natalie Abatemarco. Focus Group, November 15, 2010.
50. Denis Williams. Focus Group, June 6, 2011.
51. Louis Elneus. Focus Group, June 6, 2011.
52. Louis Elneus. Focus Group, June 6, 2011.
53. Denise Williams. Focus Group, June 6, 2011.
54. Ira Harkavy. Focus Group, November 15, 2010.
55. William Eimicke. Focus Group, November 15, 2010.
56. Ralph Smith. Focus Group, November 15, 2010.
57. William Eimicke. Focus Group, November 15, 2010.
58. John Heller. Focus Group, June 6, 2011.
59. Chong-Lim Lee. Focus Group, November 15, 2010.
60. Ibid.
61. Ralph Smith. Focus Group, November 15, 2010.
62. Ibid.
63. Ira Harkavy, Focus Group, November 15, 2010.
64. Swati Adarkar. Focus Group, November 15, 2010.
65. Ira Harkavy. Focus Group, November 15, 2010.
66. Chong-Lim Lee. Focus Group, November 15, 2010.
67. K.C. Burton. Focus Group, November 15, 2010.
68. Natalie Abatemarco. Focus Group, November 15, 2010.
69. Ira Harkavy. Focus Group, November 15, 2010.
70. Ibid.
71. Chong-Lim Lee. Focus Group, November 15, 2010.
72. Rheka Chalasani. Focus Group, June 6, 2011.
73. John Heller. Focus Group, June 6, 2011.
74. Ibid.
75. Rheka Chalasani. Focus Group, June 6, 2011.
76. John Heller. Focus Group, June 6, 2011.
77. Chong-Lim Lee. Focus Group, November 15, 2010.
78. John Heller. Focus Group, June 6, 2011.
79. William Eimicke. Focus Group, November 15, 2010.
80. Denise Williams. Focus Group, June 6, 2011.
81. Ira Harkavy. Focus Group, November 15, 2010.
82. Ibid.
83. Rheka Chalasani. Focus Group, June 6, 2011.
84. Rheka Chalasani. Focus Group, June 6, 2011.
85. UN-HABITAT (2008), *State of the World's Cities 2010/2011 – Bridging the Urban Divide*, p. x.
86. Between 40 percent and 70 percent of human-induced greenhouse gas emissions are estimated to be resulting from cities, according to UN-HABITAT's *Global Report on Human Settlements 2011 – Cities and Climate Change*, p. vi.
87. Asian Development Bank, *Urban Development*, accessed July 17, 2012 at http://www.adb.org/themes/urban-development/main.
88. UN-HABITAT (2011), *Global Report on Human Settlements 2011 – Cities and Climate Change*, p. 1.
89. UN-HABITAT (2008), *State of the World's Cities 2010/2011 – Bridging the Urban Divide*, p. x.
90. Ibid, p. xii.
91. UN-HABITAT (2008), *State of the World's Cities 2010/2011 – Bridging the Urban Divide*.
92. Ibid.

93. Ibid.
94. Brookings Institute of Metropolitan Policy Program (2010), *State of Metropolitan America*, pp. 23–4.
95. Ibid, p. 24.
96. Ibid, p. 25.
97. Ibid, p. 26.
98. Ibid, pp. 26–7.
99. William Frey (2012), *Population Growth in Metropolitan America since 1980: Putting the Volatile 2000s in Perspective*, Brookings Institute Metropolitan Policy Program, March.
100. Ibid, p. 7.
101. Ibid, pp. 7–8.
102. Ibid, p. 8.
103. Ibid, pp. 9–10.
104. Ibid, p. 12.
105. The US Conference of Mayors is the official nonpartisan organization of cities with a population of 30,000 or more, of which there are currently 1295 in the country. Each city is represented by its Mayor at the Conference.
106. The United States Conference of Mayors (2011), *Clean Energy Solutions for America's Cities*, p. 3.
107. Cleveland Foundation, *Greater University Circle: Cleveland's Urban Core*, accessed July 6, 2012 athttp://www.clevelandfoundation.org/VitalIssues/Neighbor hoodsAndHousing/GreaterUniversityCircle/.
108. Cleveland Foundation, *Greater University Circle Initiatives*, accessed July 6, 2012 at http://www.clevelandfoundation.org/VitalIssues/NeighborhoodsAnd Housing/GreaterUniversityCircle/Initiatives.html.
109. University Circle, *About-History*, accessed June 14, 2012 at http://www. universitycircle.org/about/history.
110. Cleveland Foundation, *Greater University Circle: Cleveland's Urban Core*, accessed July 6, 2012 at http://www.clevelandfoundation.org/VitalIssues/Neigh borhoodsAndHousing/GreaterUniversityCircle/.
111. www.housingpartnership.com.
112. New York City Housing Partnership, *Mission*, http://www.housingpartnership.com/.
113. Daniel Beekman (2011), "Wall Street and Federal Bucks Go to Fixing Up 'Worst Building' in the Bronx", *Daily News,* June 16.
114. For a complete list of partners, please see "Who We Are": http://www.housing partnership.com/.
115. New York City Housing Partnership, *Affiliates*, accessed at http://www.housingpart nership.com/.
116. A US incorporation status for tax-exempt nonprofit organizations.
117. International Monetary Fund (2012), *World Economic Outlook – April 2012.*
118. Ibid, p. 50.
119. OECD (May 2012) *Euro Area – Economic forecast summary*, accessed June 5, 2012 at http://www.oecd.org/document/42/0,3746,en_33873108_33873325_45268586_1_ 1_1,00.html.
120. PwC, *UK Economic Outlook March 2012*, p. 5, accessed June 6, 2012 at http:// www.pwc.co.uk/the-economy/publications/uk-economic-outlook/ukeo-july-2012- full-report.jhtml.
121. Ibid, p. 3.
122. HM Treasury (May 22, 2012) *UK Article IV Consultation 2012*", accessed June 7, 2012 at http://www.hm-treasury.gov.uk/ukecon_imf_2012.htm.
123. Local Government – Improvement and Development, Local Government Act 2000, accessed June 7, 2012 at http://www.idea.gov.uk/idk/core/page.do?pageId=71599.

124. OECD (2006), *United Kingdom (England) – Local Strategic Partnerships (LSPs)*, accessed June 7, 2012 at http://www.oecd.org/dataoecd/6/53/37728868.pdf.
125. Department for Social Development (2003), *Neighbourhood Renewal – Urban Regeneration*, accessed June 7, 2012 at http://www.dsdni.gov.uk/index/urcdg-urban_regeneration/neighbourhood_renewal.htm.
126. Local Government – Improvement and Development, *Coalition government plans – Implications for local partnership working*, accessed June 7, 2012 at http://www.idea.gov.uk/idk/core/page.do?pageId=20784973.
127. The Children and Young People's Trust, The People and Communities Forum, The Environment Forum, The Neighbourhood Forum, The Community Safety Partnership, The Health and Wellbeing Partnership, The Older People's Partnership, The Economic Regeneration Partnership.
128. McKinsey & Company (2011), *The Power of Many – Realizing the socioeconomic potential of entrepreneurs in the 21st century*, p. 28.
129. Uwe Blien and Gunther Maier (2008), *The Economics of Regional Clusters*, p. 276.
130. Ibid.
131. McKinsey & Company (2011), p. 29.
132. Uwe Blien and Gunther Maier (2008), p. 278.
133. Renewable Energy Hamburg, *About Us*, accessed November 20, 2011 at http://en.erneuerbare-energien-hamburg.de/profile.html.
134. Renewable Energy Hamburg (2011), *Swift Growth since September 2010 Launch; Hamburg's renewable energy network welcomes 100th member*, News, March 9.
135. Ibid.
136. Renewable Energy Hamburg (2011) *Renewable Energies as a Driver of Innovation and Jobs in North Germany; Successful inauguration conference of the Hamburg Renewable Energy Cluster*, News, May 26.
137. Eduard Marček and Lucia Vakulová (2005) *Cross-Sector Cooperation in Slovakia: Summary Report on the Program Implementation for the Period of 2002–2005*, accessed at http://www.partnerstva.sk..
138. Central Intelligence Agency, *The World Factbook – Slovakia*, accessed June 19, 2011 at https://www.cia.gov/library/publications/the-world-factbook/geos/lo.html.
139. Trading Economics, *Slovakia Annual GDP Growth Rate*, accessed June 19, 2011 at http://www.tradingeconomics.com/slovakia/gdp-growth-annual.
140. Marček, Eduard (2009), *This Works Here! 2% of corporate income tax allocation mechanism in Slovakia and its implications*, accessed June 19, 2011 at http://www.panet.sk/download/pres_this_works_here.pdf.
141. Marček, Eduard and Lucia Vakulová (2005).
142. Marček, Eduard (2009).
143. Dominic Wilson and Roopa Purushothaman (2006) "Dreaming with BRICs: the path to 2050", in *Emerging Economies and the Transformation of International Business – Brazil, Russia, India, and China (BRICs)*, edited by Subhash C. Jain, pp. 3–45.
144. Carlos Pereira and Joao Augusto de Castro Neves (2011), *Brazil and China: South–South Partnership or North–South Competition?* Foreign Policy at Brookings, March, accessed at http://www.brookings.edu/~/media/research/files/papers/2011/4/03%20brazil%20china%20pereira/03_brazil_china_pereira.pdf.
145. OECD (2011) *OECD Economic Surveys – Brazil (October 2011), Overview*, p. 3.
146. Ibid, p. 5.
147. OECD (2011) *OECD Economic Surveys – Russian Federation (December 2011), Overview*, p. 1.
148. Ibid, p. 16.
149. Ibid, p. 2.
150. Ibid, p. 5.

151. OECD (2012) *China in Focus: Lessons and Challenges*, p 1.
152. Ibid, p. 6.
153. Ibid, p. x.
154. Central Intelligence Agency, *The World Factbook – China,* accessed June 26, 2012 at https://www.cia.gov/library/publications/the-world-factbook/geos/ch.html.
155. OECD (2011) *OECD Economic Surveys – India (June 2011), Overview*, p. 1.
156. Ibid, p. 3.
157. Ibid, p. 1.
158. Ibid, p. 2.
159. Ibid, p. 4.
160. Central Intelligence Agency, *The World Factbook – South Africa,* accessed June 26, 2012 at https://www.cia.gov/library/publications/the-world-factbook/geos/sf.html.
161. OECD (2010) *OECD Economic Surveys – South Africa (July 2010), Overview*, p. 1.
162. James Quilligan (2002) *The Brandt Equation – 21st Century Blueprint for the New Global Economy*, p. 1.
163. World Bank, *Poverty data,* accessed June 28, 2012 at http://www.worldbank.org/en/topic/poverty.
164. Share the World's Resources (STWR) (1980), *The Brandt Report,* accessed July 4, 2012 at http://www.stwr.org/special-features/the-brandt-report.html#Dimensions.
165. Branko Milanovic (2008), *Global inequality of opportunity. How much of our income is determined at birth?* World Bank, June. Accessed July 5, 2012 at http://siteresources.worldbank.org/INTDECINEQ/Resources/Where6.pdf
166. International Energy Agency, *World Energy Outlook 2011 Factsheet,* accessed July 5, 2012 at http://www.worldenergyoutlook.org/media/weowebsite/factsheets/factsheets.pdf.
167. Shoibal Chakravarty, Ananth Chikkatur, Heleen de Coninck, Stephen Pacala, Robert Socolow, and Massimo Tavonj (2009), *Sharing global CO_2 emission reductions among one billion high emitters*, p. 1.
168. http://bhavishyaalliance.org.in/about_bhavishya_alliance.html.
169. Bhavishya Alliance, *Purpose,* accessed October 7, 2011 at http://bhavishyaalliance.org.in/aboutus.html.
170. Bhavishya Alliance, *Genesis of Bhavishya Alliance,* accessed October 7, 2011 at http://bhavishyaalliance.org.in/genesis_bhavishya_alliance.html.
171. Bhavishya Alliance, *Partners and Stakeholders,* accessed October 7, 2011 at http://bhavishyaalliance.org.in/partners_stakeholders.html.
172. Bhavishya Alliance, *Monitoring and Evaluation,* accessed October 7, 2011 at http://bhavishyaalliance.org.in/monitoring_evaluation.html.
173. Bhavishya Alliance, *Project Healthy Lokshakti – Caring for mother and child,* accessed October 7, 2011 at http://bhavishyaalliance.org.in/pdf/BA-Healthy-Lokshakti-3.pdf.
174. Bhavishya Alliance, *Behavioural Change Communications on Infant Feeding (Project Yashoda),* accessed October 7, 2011 at http://bhavishyaalliance.org.in/pdf/BA-Project-Yashada.pdf.
175. Bhavishya Alliance, *Behavioural Change on Hand Washing – Two Minutes for Optimal Hygiene,* accessed October 7, 2011 at http://bhavishyaalliance.org.in/pdf/BA-Hand-washing-3.pdf.
176. Bhavishya Alliance, *Family Based Counseling Programme,* accessed October 7, 2011 at http://bhavishyaalliance.org.in/pdf/BA-CI-4Counsellors-Programme01.pdf.
177. Ibid.
178. Bhavishya Alliance, *Food Diversification and Hygiene Education Initiative,* accessed October 7, 2011 at http://bhavishyaalliance.org.in/pdf/BA-Food-Diversification-&-Hygiene-Education-Initiative3.pdf.

179. Bhavishya Alliance, *Day Care Centres at Construction Sites Initiative*, accessed October 7, 2011 at http://bhavishyaalliance.org.in/pdf/BA-Day-Care-Centres-at-Construction-Sites-Initiative3.pdf.

180. Bhavishya Alliance, *Computer Aided Adult Literacy Health and Nutrition Awareness Program*, accessed October 7, 2011 at http://bhavishyaalliance.org.in/pdf/BA-CI-3CAALP01.pdf.

181. World Health Organization, *Tuberculosis*, accessed July 6, 2012 at http://www.who.int/mediacentre/factsheets/fs104/en/.

182. World Health Organization, *Press Conference – Launch of the Global Alliance for Anti-TB Drug Development*, accessed July 6, 2012 at http://www.who.int/director-general/speeches/2000/english/20001010_bangkok_press_conference.html.

183. Global Alliance for TB Drug Development, *Operating Model*, accessed July 6, 2012 at http://www.tballiance.org/about/operating-model.php.

184. Global Alliance for TB Drug Development, *History and Impact*, accessed July 6, 2012 at http://www.tballiance.org/about/history.php.

185. USAID China (April 2010) *Guangdong Environmental Partnership Program*, accessed at http://www.usaid.gov/rdma/documents/Guangdong%20Environmental%20Partnership_2010-08.pdf.

186. Institute for Sustainable Communities, *Who We Are*, accessed October 20, 2011 at http://www.iscvt.org/who_we_are/.

187. USAID China (April 2010).

188. Institute for Sustainable Communities (2009), *New US–China Initiative Promises to Transform Guangdong into Model for Green Development*, Press Release, May 12.

189. USAID China (April 2010)

190. Institute for Sustainable Communities, *China*, accessed October 20, 2011 at http://www.iscvt.org/where_we_work/china/.

191. CSR Wire (2009), *U.S.-China Public-Private Partnership to Green the Supply Chain*, Press Release, September 24.

192. Institute for Sustainable Communities (2009).

193. Institute for Sustainable Communities, *Environment, Health and Safety*, accessed October 21, 2011 at http://www.iscvt.org/where_we_work/china/article/ehs_academy.php.

194. Ibid.

195. CSR Wire (2009).

196. USAID China (April 2010).

197. USAID: Environmental Cooperation–Asia (2010), "Chinese Power Sector Leaders Explore U.S. Best Practices in Energy Efficiency", *USAID RDM/A Regional Environmental Office Weekly Report Week Ending October 22, 2010*, accessed October 21 2011 at http://usaid.eco-asia.org/tools/weekly_reports/news-detail.php?id=221.

198. USAID China (April 2010).

199. Institute for Sustainable Communities, *China*.

200. UN-HABITAT, Coca-Cola India. Water for Asian Cities Programme, *The Ripple Effect: Impacting Communities through Public Private Partnerships for Water and Sanitation*, accessed September 16, 2011 at http://www.unwac.org/pdf/publications/The_Ripple_Effect.pdf.

201. UN-HABITAT, *UN-HABITAT and Coca-Cola Strengthen their Partnership*, Featured Stories, News. Rio de Janero. March 23, 2010, accessed October 1, 2012 at http://www.unhabitat.org/content.asp?cid=8107&catid=7&typeid=6.

202. UN-HABITAT, Coca-Cola India. Water for Asian Cities Programme, *The Ripple Effect: Impacting Communities through Public Private Partnerships for Water and Sanitation*.

203. Ibid.

204. WASH News Asia & Pacific, *Nepal, Lalitpur: Three Communities Declared as Safe Water Zone*, July 31, 2009 accessed at http://washasia.wordpress.com/tag/coca-cola/.
205. UN-HABITAT, Coca-Cola India. Water for Asian Cities Programme, *The Ripple Effect: Impacting Communities through Public Private Partnerships for Water and Sanitation*.
206. African Union, *Rural Economy & Agriculture*, accessed July 12, 2012 at http://au.int/en/dp/rea/division/AFSD.
207. CAADP, *About CAADP*, accessed July 12, 2012 at http://www.nepad-caadp.net/about-caadp.php.
208. Grow Africa, *Ethiopia and Agricultural Investment*, accessed July 12, 2012 at http://growafrica.com/initiative/ethiopia.
209. Southern Agricultural Corridor of Tanzania, accessed July 12, 2012 at http://www.sagcot.com/.
210. Grow Africa, *Tanzania and Agricultural Investment*, accessed July 12, 2012 at http://growafrica.com/initiative/tanzania.
211. Grow Africa, *Kenya and Agricultural Investment*, accessed July 12, 2012 at http://growafrica.com/initiative/tanzania.
212. International Fund for Agricultural Development (IFAD) (2010), *Rural Poverty Report 2011*, p. iii.
213. World Bank (2007) *World Development Report 2008 – Agriculture for Development*, p. 45.
214. IFAD (2010), p. 35.
215. World Bank (2007), p. 45.
216. IFAD (2010), p. 38.
217. World Resources Institute (May 2009) *Enabling Adaptation: Priorities for Supporting the Rural Poor in a Changing Climate – WRI Issue Brief*, p. 2.
218. American Petroleum Initiative (November 10, 2006), *Angola Partnership Initiative Launched*, accessed October 27, 2011 at http://www.api.org/ehs/partnerships/community/angola-partnership.cfm
219. Fernando Paiva (2010), *Angola Partnership Initiative: Corporate Governance and Responsibility through Partnership*, Houston Major Capital Projects. Chevron Global Upstream and Gas.
220. USAID Angola, *Supporting Municipal Development in Angola*, accessed October 27, 2011 at http://www.usaid.gov/ao/business_municipal.html.
221. USAID Angola, *USAID, Chevron and the Ministry of Agricultural and Rural Development Sign Memorandum of Understanding*, accessed October 27, 2011 at http://www.usaid.gov/ao/news_articles/adfp_mou.html.
222. Chevron Corporation (March 2011) *Angola Fact Sheet*, accessed October 27, 2011 at http://www.chevron.com/documents/pdf/angolafactsheet.pdf.
223. Ibid.
224. Synergos, *Aboriginal Leadership Initiative*, accessed November 2, 2011 at http://www.synergos.org/partnerships/aboriginalleadershipcanada.htm.
225. Ahp-cii-uk, *Welcome to Ahp-cii-uk*, accessed November 2, 2011 at http://www.weavingrelationships.org/home.
226. Synergos website, see n. 224.
227. Ahp-cii-uk website, see n. 225.
228. Ahp-cii-uk, *Tsheshaht*, accessed November 2, 2011 at http://www.weavingrelationships.org/tseshaht.
229. Ibid.
230. Ahp-cii-uk, *Ehattesaht*, accessed November 2, 2011 at http://www.weavingrelationships.org/ehattesaht .

231. Ahp-cii-uk, *Ahousaht*, accessed November 2, 2011 at http://www.weaving relationships.org/ahousaht.
232. United Nations Environment Programme (2012) *GEO 5 – Global Environment Outlook. Environment for the future we want*, p. 5.
233. Janet L. Swin and William R. Moomaw (2009), *Renewable Revolution: Low-Carbon Energy by 2030*, p. 5.
234. World Meteorological Organization (2011) *WMO Greenhouse Gas Bulletin – No. 7\November 2011*, p. 1.
235. Data from 2009, as cited in International Energy Agency (2011), *CO_2 Emissions from Fuel Combustion – Highlights\2011 Edition*.
236. Ibid, p. 9.
237. Ibid, p 10.
238. British Petroleum (2012), *BP Statistical Review of World Energy | June 2012*, p. 2.
239. International Energy Agency (2011), p. 11.
240. United Nations Industrial Development organization, South Africa, *Durban Industry Climate Change Partnership Project*, accessed June 28, 2011 at http://www.unido.org/index.php?id=1000128.
241. United Nations Industrial Development Organization, Project No: YA/INT/08/A09, *Climate Change Mitigation of Industrial Activity through Investment and Technology Compacts and Partnerships – Durban, South Africa and China Work Plan*, accessed June 28, 2011 at http://www.unido.org/fileadmin/user_media/UNIDO_Worldwide/Offices/UNIDO_Offices/South_Africa/ClimatChangePartnership Summary.pdf.
242. http://www.warwickshire.gov.uk/climatechangepartnership.
243. Energy and Climate Change Partnership of the Americas, *About ECPA*, accessed November 20, 2011 at http://ecpamericas.org/About-ECPA.aspx .
244. Energy and Climate Change Partnership of the Americas, *Initiatives*, accessed November 20, 2011 at http://ecpamericas.org/initiatives/default.aspx .
245. Energy and Climate Change Partnership of the Americas, *Central American Energy and Environmental Security Initiative (ESSI)*, accessed November 20, 2011 at http://ecpamericas.org/initiatives/default.aspx?id=22.
246. Energy and Climate Change Partnership of the Americas, *Chile Renewable Energy Center*, accessed November 20, 2011 at http://ecpamericas.org/initiatives/default.aspx?id=23.
247. Energy and Climate Change Partnership of the Americas, *ECPA Caribbean Initiative*, accessed November 20, 2011 at http://ecpamericas.org/initiatives/default.aspx?id=25.
248. Energy and Climate Change Partnership of the Americas, *Lighting the Americas*, accessed November 20, 2011 at http://ecpamericas.org/initiatives/default.aspx?id=30.
249. Energy and Climate Change Partnership of the Americas, *Peace Corps Renewable Energy and Climate Change Initiative*, accessed November 20, 2011 at http://ecpamericas.org/initiatives/default.aspx?id=35.
250. Energy and Climate Change Partnership of the Americas, *USTDA Clean Energy Exchange Program of the Americas*, accessed November 20, 2011 at http://ecpamericas.org/initiatives/default.aspx?id=38.
251. World Health Organization (2010), *World Heath Report (2010) – Executive Summary*, p. 9.
252. Ibid, p. 8.
253. Ibid, p. 9.
254. World Health Organization (2002), *World Heath Report 2002 – Reducing Risks, Promoting Healthy Life*, p. 7.
255. www.sm2015.org.

256. Inter-American Development Bank (2010), *Bill & Melinda Gates Foundation, Carlos Slim Health Institute, Spain, and the IDB Collaborate to Improve Health of the Poor in Mesoamerica*, News Releases, June 14.
257. Salud Mesoamérica 2015, accessed July 15, 2011 at http://www.sm2015.org.
258. Tristao, I. (2011), *Perfiles de los Países Mesoamericanos*, accessed October 1, 2012 at http://gtrvidasmaternas.org/GTR/sites/default/files/SM2015%20Documento%20 de%20Proyecto%20Abril%2030%202011%20ESP_0.pdf.
259. Dr. Emma Margarita Iriarte. Email, 30 November, 2011.
260. SM2015 M&E Plan, Interamerican Development Bank. Accessed via Dr. E.M. Iriarte, 30 November, 2011.
261. Dr. Emma Margarita Iriarte. Telephone interview, 30 November, 2011; Project Document, *Salud Mesoamérica 2015*, 22 August, 2011. Accessed via Dr. E.M. Iriarte, 30 November, 2011.
262. Dr. Emma Margarita Iriarte. Telephone interview, 30 November, 2011.
263. http://www.theaccessproject.com/index.php/home/.
264. Key partners: Millennium Villages, The Global Network for Tropical Disease Control, Rwanda Works, Rwandan Ministry of Health, Malaria No More, The Center for Global Health and Economic Development, The Earth Institute, Elizabeth Glazer Pediatric AIDS Foundation, Dian Fossey Gorilla Fund International, Global Fund to Fight AIDS, Tuberculosis and Malaria, IntraHealth, Pfizer Global Health Fellows Program, Peace Corps, and Global Health Corps.
265. http://www.pfizer.com/responsibility/global_health/international_trachoma_ initiative.jsp.
266. Pfizer, "Partnership to End Blinding Trachoma through the International Trachoma Initiative", *Doing Business Responsibly*, accessed July 8, 2011 at http:// www.pfizer.com/responsibility/global_health/international_trachoma_initiative.jsp.
267. Pfizer Investment in Health, *Partnership to End Blinding Trachoma: The International Trachoma Initiative (ITI)*, accessed July 8, 2011 at http://www.pfizer.com/ files/philanthropy/International_Trachoma_Initiative_factsheet.pdf.
268. PQMD Case Study, *Pfizer Donates Zithromax in Fight to Eliminate Trachoma*, accessed July 8, 2011 at http://www.pqmd.org/cms/node/115.
269. World Bank, *Poverty*, accessed July 20, 2012 at http://www.worldbank.org/en/topic/ poverty.
270. OECD (2011), *An Overview of Growing Income Inequalities in OECD Countries: Main Findings* for *Divided We Stand: Why Inequality Keeps Rising*, p. 22.
271. OECD (2011), "Special Focus: Inequality in Emerging Economies (EEs)" for *Divided We Stand: Why Inequality Keeps Rising*, p. 49.
272. The report is based on data from the 2011 Current Population Survey Annual Social and Economic Supplement (CPS ASEC), collected in the 50 states and the District of Columbia.
273. Carmen DeNavas-Walt, Bernadette D. Proctor, and Jessica C. Smith (2011), *Income, Poverty, and Health Insurance Coverage in the United States: 2010*, p. 14.
274. www.millenniumpromise.org.
275. United Nations, *Millennium Development Goals*, http://www.un.org/ millenniumgoals/.
276. For a complete list of partners, please see: http://millenniumvillages.org/about/our-partners/.
277. http://www.africacorridors.com/sagcot/index.php.
278. Agricultural Council of Tanzania, *The Kilimo Kwanza Resolution*, Accessed July 26, 2011 at http://www.actanzania.org/index.php?option=com_content&task=view&id= 121&Itemid=39.
279. Deogratias Mushi (2011), "Sagcot Initiative – Shot in the Arm for Local Farmers", *Tanzania Daily News*, January 31.

280. Ibid.
281. The Agricultural Council of Tanzania is an umbrella organization of the agriculture private sector in Tanzania. AgDevCo is a nonprofit organization that invests in "social venture capital" to create commercially viable agribusiness opportunities in Africa. Prorustica is a consulting firm that specializes in fostering growth in agricultural commodity markets and in creating public private partnerships.
282. Patrick Guyver. Telephone interview, 8 November, 2011.
283. Patrick Guyver. Telephone interview, 8 November, 2011.
284. The full text of the report is not yet available on SAGCOT's website as of July 26, 2011.
285. Deogratias Mushi (2011).
286. Chris Isaac (2011), *SAGCOT Investment Blueprint: Key Messages,*. SAGCOT; AgDevCo, accessed at http://www.agdevco.com/sysimages/sagcot_ibp_launch_rpt1.pdf.
287. Deogratias Mushi (2011).
288. Patrick Guyver. Telephone interview, 8 November 2011.
289. Ralph Smith. Focus Group, November 15, 2010.
290. Natalie Abatemarco. Focus Group, November 15, 2010.
291. Ira Harkavy. Focus Group, November 15, 2010.
292. Ibid.
293. Ralph Smith. Focus Group, November 15, 2010.
294. Chong-Lim Lee. Focus Group, November 15, 2010.
295. Ralph Smith. Focus Group, November 15, 2010.
296. Denise William. Focus Group, June 6, 2011.
297. Louis Elneus. Focus Group, June 6, 2011.
298. Rheka Chalasani. Focus Group, June 6, 2011.
299. Louis Elneus. Focus Group, June 6, 2011.
300. Ibid.
301. Rheka Chalasani. Focus Group, June 6, 2011.
302. John Heller. Focus Group, June 6, 2011.
303. www.wagner.edu/cls/prp/.

References

African Union, *Rural Economy & Agriculture*, accessed July 12, 2012 at http://au.int/en/dp/rea/division/AFSD.

Agricultural Council of Tanzania, accessed July 26, 2011 at http://www.actanzania.org/index.php?option=com_content&task=view&id=121&Itemid=39.

Ahp-cii-uk, accessed November 2, 2011 at http://www.weavingrelationships.org/home.

American Petroleum Initiative (2006), *Angola Partnership Initiative Launched*, accessed October 27, 2011 at http://www.api.org/ehs/partnerships/community/angola-partnership.cfm.

Andrews, Rhys and Tom Entwistle (2010), "Does Cross-Sectoral Partnership Deliver? An Empirical Exploration of Public Service Effectiveness, Efficiency, and Equity", *Journal of Public Administration Research and Theory* 20 (January).

Asian Development Bank (2008), *Public–Private Partnership Handbook*, accessed at http://www.adb.org/sites/default/files/pub/2008/Public-Private-Partnership.pdf.

Asian Development Bank, *Urban Development*, accessed July 17, 2012 at http://www.adb.org/themes/urban-development/main.

Austin, James E. (2000), *The Collaboration Challenge: How Nonprofits and Businesses Succeed Through Strategic Alliances*, New York: the Peter F. Drucker Foundation for Nonprofit Management.

Beekman, Daniel (2011), "Wall Street and Federal Bucks Go to Fixing Up 'Worst Building' in the Bronx", *Daily News*, June 16.

Bhavishya Alliance, accessed October 7, 2011 at http://bhavishyaalliance.org.in/.

Blien, Uwe and Gunther Maier (2008), *The Economics of Regional Clusters*, Cheltenham, UK and Northampton, MA, USA: Edward Elgar Publishing.

Branzei, Oana and Marlene J. Le Ber (2010), "Towards a Critical Theory of Value Creation in Cross-Sector Partnerships", *Organization* 17.

British Petroleum (2012), *Statistical Review of World Energy*, accessed at http://www.bp.com/assets/bp_internet/globalbp/globalbp_uk_english/reports_and_publications/statistical_energy_review_2011/STAGING/local_assets/pdf/statistical_review_of_world_energy_full_report_2012.pdf.

Brookings Institute of Metropolitan Policy Program (2010), *State of Metropolitan America*, accessed at http://www.brookings.edu/~/media/Research/Files/Reports/2010/5/09%20metro%20america/metro_america_report.pdf.

Bryson, John M., Barbara C. Crosby, and Melissa Middleton Stone (2006), "The Design and Implementation of Cross-Sector Collaborations: Propositions from the Literature", *Public Administration Review* 66 (December).

Central Intelligence Agency, *The World Factbook*, accessed June 26, 2012 at https://www.cia.gov/library/publications/the-world-factbook/index.html.

Chakravarty, Shoibal, Ananth Chikkatur, Heleen de Coninck, Stephen Pacala, Robert Socolow, and Massimo Tavonj (2009), "Sharing Global CO_2 Emission Reductions Among One Billion High Emitters", *PNAS Early Edition*.

Chevron Corporation (2011), *Angola Fact Sheet*, accessed October 2011 at http://www.chevron.com/documents/pdf/angolafactsheet.pdf.

City of New York (2009), *Inventory of New York City Greenhouse Gas Emissions, September 2009*, accessed at http://nytelecom.vo.llnwd.net/o15/agencies/planyc2030/pdf/greenhousegas_2009.pdf.

City of San Jose (2007), *San Jose's Green Vision*, accessed at http://www.sanjoseca.gov/pdf/sanjosegreenvision.pdf.

City of San Jose (2011), *Green Vision 2011 Annual Report*, accessed at http://www.sanjoseca.gov/clerk/Agenda/20120320/20120320_0303att.pdf.

Cleveland Foundation, accessed July 6, 2012 at http://www.clevelandfoundation.org/.

Clinton Global Initiative, accessed July 13, 2012 at http://www.clintonglobalinitiative.org/.

The Comprehensive African Agricultural Development Programme (CAADP), accessed July 12, 2012 at http://www.nepad-caadp.net/.

CSR Wire (2009), *U.S.-China Public-Private Partnership to Green the Supply Chain*, Press Release, September 24.

DeNavas-Walt, Carmen, Bernadette D. Proctor, and Jessica C. Smith (2011), *Income, Poverty, and Health Insurance Coverage in the United States: 2010*, Washington, DC: U.S. Department of Commerce, Economics and Statistics Administration, US Census Bureau, accessed at http://www.census.gov/prod/2010pubs/p60-238.pdf.

Department for Social Development (2003), *Neighbourhood Renewal – Urban Regeneration*, accessed June 7, 2012 at http://www.dsdni.gov.uk/index/urcdg-urban_regeneration/neighbourhood_renewal.htm.

Energy and Climate Change Partnership of the Americas, accessed November 20, 2011 at http://ecpamericas.org/About-ECPA.aspx.

Frey, William (2012), *Population Growth in Metropolitan America since 1980: Putting the Volatile 2000s in Perspective*, Brookings Institute Metropolitan Policy Program, accessed at http://www.brookings.edu/~/media/research/files/papers/2012/3/20%20population%20frey/0320_population_frey.

Geddes, Michael (2005), *Making Public/Private Partnerships Work: Building Relationships and Understanding Cultures*, Aldershot, UK: Gower Publishing Limited.

Glasbergen, Pieter, Frank Biermann, and Arthur P.J. Mol (2007), *Partnerships, Governance, and Sustainable Development*, Cheltenham, UK and Northampton, MA, USA: Edward Elgar Publishing.

Global Alliance for TB Drug Development, accessed July 6, 2012 at http://www.tballiance.org/.

Googins, Bradley K. and Steven A. Rochlin (2000), "Creating the Partnership Society: Understanding the Rhetoric and Reality of Cross-Sectoral Partnerships", *Business and Society Review* 105:1 (Spring).

Grow Africa, accessed July 12, 2012 at http://growafrica.com/.

HM Treasury, *UK Article IV Consultation 2012*, accessed June 7, 2012 at http://www.hm-treasury.gov.uk/ukecon_imf_2012.htm.

Hodge, Graeme and Carsten Greve, eds. (2005), *The Challenge of Public Private Partnerships: Learning from International Experience*, Cheltenham, UK and Northampton, MA, USA: Edward Elgar Publishing.

Institute for Sustainable Communities (2009), *New US–China Initiative Promises to Transform Guangdong into Model for Green Development*, Press Release, May 12.

Intern-American Development Bank (2010), "Bill & Melinda Gates Foundation, Carlos Slim Health Institute, Spain, and the IDB Collaborate to Improve the Health of the Poor in Mesoamerica", News Release, June 14.

International Energy Agency (2011), CO_2 *Emissions from Fuel Combustion – Highlights*, Paris: OECD/IEA, accessed at http://www.iea.org/co2highlights/co2highlights.pdf.

International Energy Agency, *World Energy Outlook 2011 Factsheet*, accessed July 5, 2012 at http://www.worldenergyoutlook.org/media/weowebsite/factsheets/factsheets.pdf.

International Fund for Agricultural Development (2010), *Rural Poverty Report 2011*, accessed at http://www.ifad.org/rpr2011/report/e/rpr2011.pdf.

International Monetary Fund (2012), *World Economic Outlook – April 2012*, accessed at http://www.imf.org/external/pubs/ft/weo/2012/01/pdf/text.pdf.

Isaac, Chris (2011), *SAGCOT Investment Blueprint: Key Messages*, SAGCOT; AgDevCo, accessed at http://www.agdevco.com/sysimages/sagcot_ibp_launch_rpt1.pdf.

Klaus, Grebmer, Frank Hartwich, and David J. Spielman (2010), "Public-Private Partnerships and Developing-Country Agriculture: Evidence from the International Agricultural Research System", *Public Administration and Development* 30:4.

Le Ber, Marlene J. and Oana Branzei (2010), "(Re)Forming Strategic Cross-Sector Partnerships: Relational Processes of Social Innovation", *Business & Society* 49:1.

Link, Albert N. (2006), *Public/Private Partnerships: Innovation and Strategies and Policy Alternatives*, New York: Springer Science and Media, Inc.

Local Government – Improvement and Development, accessed June 7, 2012 at http://www.idea.gov.uk/idk/core/page.do?pageId=1.

Marček, Eduard (2009), *This Works Here! 2% of Corporate Income Tax Allocation Mechanism in Slovakia and its Implications*, accessed June 19, 2011 at http://www.panet.sk/download/pres_this_works_here.pdf

Marček, Eduard and Lucia Vakulová (2005), *Cross-Sector Cooperation in Slovakia: Summary Report on the Program Implementation for the Period of 2002–2005*, accessed at http://www.partnerstva.sk.

Maurrasse, David (2001), *Beyond the Campus: How Colleges and Universities Form Partnerships with their Communities*, New York: Routledge.

McKinsey & Company (2011), *The Power of Many – Realizing the Socio-economic Potential of Entrepreneurs in the 21st Century*, accessed at http://g20yes2011.files.wordpress.com/2011/10/the-power-of-many-mckinsey-report-20110310.pdf.

Milanovic, Branko (2008), *Global Inequality of Opportunity. How Much of our Income is Determined at Birth?* World Bank, June, accessed at http://site resources.worldbank.org/INTDECINEQ/Resources/Where6.pdf.

Mushi, Deogratias (2011), "Sagcot Initiative – Shot in the Arm for Local Farmers", *Tanzania Daily News*, January 31.

New York City Housing Partnership, accessed at http://www.housing partnership.com/.

OECD (2006), *United Kingdom (England) – Local Strategic Partnerships (LSPs)*, accessed June 7, 2012 at http://www.oecd.org/dataoecd/6/53/377 28868.pdf.

OECD (2010), *OECD Economic Surveys – South Africa (July 2010), Overview*, accessed at http://www.oecd.org/economy/economicsurveysandcountrysurveil lance/45650043.pdf.

OECD (2011), 'An Overview of Growing Income Inequalities in OECD Countries: Main Findings', for *Divided We Stand: Why Inequality Keeps Rising*, accessed at http://www.oecd.org/els/socialpoliciesanddata/49499779.pdf.

OECD (2011), 'Special Focus: Inequality in Emerging Economies (EEs)', for *Divided We Stand: Why Inequality Keeps Rising*, accessed at http:// www.oecd.org/social/socialpoliciesanddata/49170475.pdf.

OECD (2011), *OECD Economic Surveys – Brazil (October 2011), Overview*, accessed at http://www.oecd.org/economy/economicsurveysandcountrysurveil lance/48930900.pdf.

OECD (2011), *OECD Economic Surveys – India (June 2011), Overview*, accessed at http://www.oecd.org/eco/48108317.pdf.

OECD (2011), *OECD Economic Surveys – Russian Federation (December 2011), Overview*, accessed at http://www.oecd.org/eco/49207915.pdf.

OECD (2012), *China in Focus: Lessons and Challenges*, accessed at http:// www.oecd.org/china/50011051.pdf

OECD (2012), *Euro Area – Economic Forecast Summary*, accessed June 5, 2012 at http://www.oecd.org/document/42/0,3746,en_33873108_33873325_4526 8586_1_1_1,00.html.

OECD.StatExtracts, *Central Government Debt*, accessed July 10, 2012 at http:// stats.oecd.org/Index.aspx?datasetcode=GOV_DEBT#.

Paiva, Fernando (2010), *Angola Partnership Initiative: Corporate Governance and Responsibility through Partnership*, Houston Major Capital Projects, ChevronGlobal Upstream and Gas.

Pereira, Carlos and Joao Augusto de Castro Neves (2011), *Brazil and China: South–South Partnership or North–South Competition?* Foreign Policy at Brookings, March, accessed at http://www.brookings.edu/~/media/research/ files/papers/2011/4/03%20brazil%20china%20pereira/03_brazil_china_ pereira.pdf.

Pfizer (2011), *Partnership to End Blinding Trachoma through the International Trachoma Initiative*, accessed July 8, 2011 at http://www.pfizer.com/ responsibility/global_health/international_trachoma_initiative.jsp.

Porter, Oliver W. (2008), *Public/Private Partnerships for Local Government*, Bloomington, IN: Authorhouse.

PwC (2012), *UK Economic Outlook March 2012*, accessed at http://www.pwc.co.uk/the-economy/publications/uk-economic-outlook/ukeo-july-2012-full-report.jhtml.

Quilligan, James (2002), *The Brandt Equation – 21st Century Blueprint for the New Global Economy*, Philadelphia: Brandt 21 Forum, accessed at http://www.brandt21forum.info/BrandtEquation-19Sept04.pdf.

Renewable Energy Hamburg, accessed at http://en.erneuerbare-energien-hamburg.de/profile.html.

Rogerson, Christian M. (2010), "In Search of Public-Private Sector Partnerships for Local Development in South Africa", *Urban Forum* 21.

Rondinelli, Dennis A. and Ted London (2003), "How Corporations and Environmental Groups Cooperate: Assessing Cross-Sector Alliances and Collaborations", *Academy of Management Executive* 17:23.

Salud Mesoamérica 2015, accessed July 15, 2011 at http://www.sm2015.org.

Selsky, John W. and Barbara Parker (2005), "Cross-Sector Partnerships to Address Social Issues: Challenges to Theory and Practice", *Journal of Management* 31:6 (December).

Share the World's Resources (STWR) (1980), The Brandt Report, accessed July 4, 2012 at http://www.stwr.org/special-features/the-brandt-report.html#Dimensions.

Swin, Janet L. and William R. Moomaw (2009), *Renewable Revolution: Low-Carbon Energy by 2030*, Worldwatch Institute.

Trading Economics, *Slovakia Annual GDP Growth Rate*, accessed June 19, 2011 at http://www.tradingeconomics.com/slovakia/gdp-growth-annual.

Tristao, I. (2011), Perfiles de los Países Mesoamericanos, accessed October 1, 2012 at http://gtrvidasmaternas.org/GTR/sites/default/files/SM2015%20Documento%20de%20Proyecto%20Abril%2030%202011%20ESP_0.pdf.

UN-HABITAT, Coca-Cola India, Water for Asian Cities Programme, *The Ripple Effect: Impacting Communities through Public Private Partnerships for Water and Sanitation*, accessed September 16, 2011 at http://www.unwac.org/pdf/publications/The_Ripple_Effect.pdf.

United Nations (2011), *The Millennium Development Goals Report*, accessed at http://www.un.org/millenniumgoals/11_MDG%20Report_EN.pdf.

United Nations Department of Economic and Social Affairs (2009), *World Population Ageing 2009*, accessed at http://www.un.org/esa/population/publications/WPA2009/WPA2009_WorkingPaper.pdf.

United Nations Environment Programme (2012), *GEO 5 – Global Environment Outlook. Environment for the Future we Want*, accessed at http://www.unep.org/geo/pdfs/geo5/GEO5_report_full_en.pdf.

United Nations Human Settlements Programme (2008), *State of the World's Cities 2010/2011 – Bridging the Urban Divide*, accessed at http://www.unhabitat.org/pmss/listItemDetails.aspx?publicationID=2917.

United Nations Human Settlements Programme (2011), *Global Report on Human Settlements 2011 – Cities and Climate Change*, accessed at http://www.unhabitat.org/pmss/listItemDetails.aspx?publicationID=3086.

United Nations Industrial Development Organization (2009), *Climate Change Mitigation of Industrial Activity through Investment and Technology Compacts and Partnerships – Durban, South Africa and China Work Plan*, accessed at http://www.unido.org/fileadmin/user_media/UNIDO_Worldwide/Offices/ UNIDO_Offices/South_Africa/ClimatChangePartnershipSummary.pdf

United Nations Population Fund (2007), *State of World Population 2007 – Unleashing the Potential of Urban Growth*, accessed at http://www.unfpa.org/ swp/2007/presskit/pdf/sowp2007_eng.pdf.

United Nations, *We Can End Poverty 2015 Millennium Development Goals*, accessed July 13, 2012 at http://www.un.org/millenniumgoals/.

The United States Conference of Mayors (2011), *Clean Energy Solutions for America's Cities*, accessed at http://usmayors.org/cleanenergy/report.pdf.

University Circle, accessed June 14, 2012 at http://www.universitycircle.org/.

USAID Angola, *USAID, Chevron and Ministry of Agricultural and Rural Development Sign Memorandum of Understanding,* accessed October 27, 2011 at http://www.usaid.gov/ao/news_articles/adfp_mou.html.

USAID China (2010), *Guangdong Environmental Partnership Program*, accessed at http://www.usaid.gov/rdma/documents/Guangdong%20Environmental%20 Partnership_2010-08.pdf.

USAID: Environmental Cooperation–Asia (2010), "Chinese Power Sector Leaders Explore U.S. Best Practices in Energy Efficiency", *USAID RDM/A Regional Environmental Office Weekly Report Week Ending October 22, 2010*, accessed October 21, 2011 at http://usaid.eco-asia.org/tools/weekly_reports/ news-detail.php?id=221.

Vaillancourt Rosenau, Pauline, ed. (2000), *Public/Private Policy Partnerships*, Cambridge, MA: Massachusetts Institute of Technology.

Vollmer, Derek, National Research Council (2009), *Enhancing the Effectiveness of Sustainability Partnerships*, Washington, DC: The National Academies Press.

WASH News Asia & Pacific (2009), *Nepal, Lalitpur: Three Communities Declared as Safe Water Zone*, posted on July 31, 2009, accessed at http:// washasia.wordpress.com/tag/coca-cola/.

Wilson, Dominic and Roopa Purushothaman (2006), "Dreaming with BRICs: The Path to 2050", in Subhash C. Jain, ed., *Emerging Economies and the Transformation of International Business – Brazil, Russia, India, and China (BRICs)*, Cheltenham, UK and Northampton, MA, USA: Edward Elgar Publishing.

World Bank (2007), *World Development Report 2008 – Agriculture for Development*, accessed at http://siteresources.worldbank.org/INTWDR2008/Resources/ WDR_00_book.pdf.

World Bank, *Poverty*, accessed July 20, 2012 at http://www.worldbank.org/en/ topic/poverty.

World Economic Forum, accessed July 13, 2012 at http://www.weforum.org/ members.

World Health Organization (2000), *World Population Ageing 2009 Press Conference – Launch of the Global Alliance for Anti-TB Drug Development*, accessed July 6, 2012 at http://www.who.int/director-general/speeches/2000/ english/20001010_bangkok_press_conference.html.

World Health Organization (2002), *World Heath Report 2002 – Reducing Risks, Promoting Healthy Life*, accessed at http://epsl.asu.edu/ceru/Documents/whr_ overview_eng.pdf.

World Health Organization (2010), *World Heath Report (2010) – Executive Summary*, accessed at http://www.who.int/whr/2010/10_summary_en.pdf.

World Health Organization, accessed July 6, 2012 at http://www.who.int/.

World Meteorological Organization (2011), *WMO Greenhouse Gas Bulletin – No. 7, November 2011*, accessed at http://www.wmo.int/pages/mediacentre/press_releases/documents/GHGbulletin.pdf.

World Resources Institute (2009), *Enabling Adaptation: Priorities for Supporting the Rural Poor in a Changing Climate – WRI Issue Brief. May 2009*, accessed at http://pdf.wri.org/issue_brief_enabling_adaptation.pdf.

Index